THE HOLLOW STATE

POWER WITHOUT PURPOSE IN AUSTRALIAN POLITICS

PETER VAN ONSELEN

Published by:
Wilkinson Publishing Pty Ltd
ACN 006 042 173
PO Box 24135
Melbourne, Vic 3001
Ph: 03 9654 5446

enquiries@wilkinsonpublishing.com.au
www.wilkinsonpublishing.com.au

Title: The Hollow State

ISBN: 9781921804724

A catalogue record for this book is available from the National Library of Australia.

Cover design and internal design by Spike Creative

Printed and bound in Australia by Ligare Book Printers.

CONTENTS

ABOUT THE AUTHOR

Dr Peter van Onselen is an Australian academic, author and commentator. He is currently Professor of Politics and Public Policy in the Business School at The University of Western Australia (UWA), and the Political Editor at Daily Mail Australia.

From 2009-2024, Peter was the Contributing Editor at *The Australian* newspaper, where he also wrote a weekly column in the *Weekend Australian*. Peter was the Political Editor at Network 10 from 2018-2023, co-hosting *The Sunday Project* with Lisa Wilkinson and The Professor & The Hack podcast with Hugh Riminton during his time at the network.

From 2010 to 2017, Peter hosted news and politics programs on Sky News Australia, including the daily lunchtime program *To the Point*, with former NSW Premier Kristina Keneally, and Sky's flagship Sunday morning political interview program *Australian Agenda*, with *The Australian* newspaper's editor-at-large Paul Kelly.

Peter has won Walkley and Logie awards for his broadcast journalism (at both Sky News and Network 10) and a News Awards for his print commentary in *The Australian*.

Peter has authored ten books. His best-selling biography of John Howard was rated by *The Wall Street Journal* as the best biography of 2007. During his 20-year academic career, Peter has served as the foundation chair of journalism at UWA, professor of politics and public policy at Griffith University and associate professor and head of discipline in government and politics at Edith Cowan University.

Peter holds a PhD in political science (UWA), a masters in commerce (CSU), a masters in policy studies (UNSW) and a Bachelor of Arts with first class honours in political science and a major in philosophy (UNSW).

He is a fellow at the UWA Institute of Public Policy, a member of the Australian Economic Society, the Australasian Political Studies Association and an ambassador for the Australian Indigenous Education Foundation, having previously served on the board of Teach for Australia.

INTRODUCTION

This is a book about the absence of purpose within politics. Not the collapse of institutions, but the slow erosion of what once animated them. Australia today is governed not by tyrants or ideologues, but by managers. We are not suffering from chaos or authoritarianism, but from something more insidious: a system that performs the rituals of democracy without embodying its values. That is the essence of the hollow state.

A hollow state is not a failed state. Services are still delivered, laws are still passed, governments change, parliaments sit and budgets are handed down. But increasingly, there is a sense that none of it means very much anymore. The machinery still runs, but it runs on empty. Political leaders have titles but little authority to meaningfully perform their role. Parties have logos but fewer and fewer members in an era of political professionalisation. Public servants occupy offices but are denied the space (and freedom) to think as well as the independence to question. The media reports, but it rarely challenges, at least not with depth and purpose. The system functions, technically speaking, but it no longer inspires, leads, or renews the way it once did.

This book takes that hollowness seriously, examining the way in which our political system has become performative rather than purposeful. It looks at how the rise of the political class, the decline of party democracy, the weakening of the public service, and the shrinking of serious journalism have all contributed to a democratic order that looks intact but is increasingly devoid of real substance.

The hollow state is marked by the dominance of tactics over strategy, image over integrity, and short-term wins over long-term outcomes. It is shaped by leaders more interested in managing headlines and photo opportunities than solving problems. It is reinforced by institutions that reward caution rather than courage. It is tolerated by a media environment more invested in entertainment than accountability. And the public endures what is going on around them, understandably, growing cynical and disengaged from our democratic polity at a time when access to information should be facilitating political engagement.

This is not a uniquely Australian phenomenon. Other democracies show similar symptoms, but my focus is here. For a country that once prided itself on pioneering reforms and innovative public administration, the current malaise is rather striking. Once a laboratory of democracy, Australia now feels like a holding pattern of ever lowering expectations.

What follows in the chapters ahead is an exploration of how we got here, why it matters, and what (if anything) can be done to turn the situation around. But before we look forward, we need to look back. The hollow state didn't come out of nowhere. Its emergence has a history, shaped by decisions made over decades. It is not the result of one party or one leader, but of structural shifts that have changed how politics is done.

The hollow state did not emerge fully formed from a specific ideological shift. Rather, it developed gradually, shaped by a series of cultural, structural and institutional changes that began in the latter decades of the twentieth century and accelerated into the twenty-first. In retrospect, the signs were there early, but they were often interpreted as progress, or at least as necessary adaptation. Only with the benefit of hindsight can we see that what looked like evolution was often in fact erosion.

The origins of the hollow state can be traced back to the period leading into the Hawke government, when Australian politics was still populated by conviction politicians since Federation in 1900, ideologically grounded parties, and a relatively independent public service. But by the time the 1980s unfolded, a new kind of politics had started to take hold. The demands of the modern media, technology advances, the pressures of economic globalisation, and the rise of political staffers as a pipeline to parliamentary careers were already reshaping how politics functioned.

To be clear: this was not yet the moment of hollowing out. The Hawke and Keating governments were activist, reformist, and agenda-driven. They pursued economic modernisation with vigour and skill, engaging the bureaucracy in serious policy development and pushing reforms that redefined Australia's economic landscape. Whatever one thinks of the policies themselves, they were driven by ideas and executed with a seriousness that stands in sharp contrast to what followed not long after.

But it is precisely during this period, paradoxically rich in reform, that the conditions for the hollow state began to take shape. Since the 1980s, professionalisation crept into politics in Australia. Political parties, once mass membership organisations rooted in local branches and grassroots activism, began to shrink. Career pathways for politicians narrowed, with fewer MPs entering parliament with experience running their own small businesses or from professions like education, business or law, and more emerging from within the political system itself, as staffers, advisers or apparatchiks. The result has been a subtle but important cultural shift: politics became a profession, not a calling.

The young staffers who came of age during the Hawke-Keating era absorbed the mechanics of reform but not necessarily the motivation behind it. They saw that politics could be strategic, that messaging mattered, and that winning the media cycle could make or break a policy push. But many learned the wrong lessons. They took away tactics, not values. They saw the importance of controlling the narrative but overlooked the need for conviction. They mastered spin before ever going on to master substance. By the time some of them entered parliament themselves, often via factional machinations rather than grassroots support, they brought with them a hollowed-out conception of political life, focused on process, branding and self-preservation. This continued amongst some of the also-rans and apparatchiks working within the Howard government (1996-2007).

Meanwhile, other pillars of democratic governance were undergoing their own transformations. The public service, once a repository of institutional memory and independent policy expertise, began to feel the weight of politicisation. This, too, began in the 1980s, accelerating in the 1990s and beyond, as governments sought greater responsiveness from departments and insisted on loyalty alongside competence. The introduction of the Senior Executive Service, performance contracts, and a growing cohort of ministerial advisers altered the balance of power between elected officials and career bureaucrats. Over time, frank and fearless advice gave way to calculated caution, and departments became more inclined to tell ministers what they wanted to hear rather than what they needed to know. The long-term result has been a bureaucracy increasingly risk-averse, less policy-driven, and more willing to accommodate political imperatives at the expense of the public interest.

At the same time the media, traditionally referred to as the fourth estate and playing a watchdog role over both government and opposition, began its own transition. Again, the changes were incremental but in time significant. As traditional business models faltered in the face of digital disruption, newsrooms shrank.

Journalistic expertise was lost. Resources to cover politics seriously and follow policy debates in depth, to fact-check political spin and to hold power to account all diminished. Coverage became more reactive, more driven by spectacle and more focused on personalities than policies. The line between news and entertainment blurred. Politicians adapted quickly, becoming ever more skilled at manipulating the media cycle, feeding journalists with (sometimes) manufactured controversies, and using social media to bypass scrutiny altogether. The net result is a media landscape less capable of (and often less interested in) probing the substance of government.

Each of these developments: the professionalisation of politics, the weakening of the public service and the decline of serious journalism, may have seemed manageable or even benign in isolation. But together, they created a dangerous synergy. Politics became less about ideas and more about image. Governments became more obsessed with announcements than outcomes. Policy drifted while spin dominated. Public trust, predictably, began to erode.

The Howard years (1996–2007) crystallised this shift. While John Howard was a conviction politician in his own right, and his government pursued a clear ideological agenda in some areas, he also institutionalised many of the managerialist tendencies that came to define the hollow state. Howard mastered the permanent campaign. His government tightened control over the public service, expanded the role of political advisers, and perfected the art of tactical policy-making. Importantly, Howard's long tenure normalised the idea that politics was about managing rather than transforming, about winning the next election rather than planning for the next generation. In doing so, he cemented a template that future governments, Labor and Liberal alike, would adopt from and expand on.

The post-Howard era, marked by leadership instability, policy backflips, and an increasingly cynical public, saw the hollow state develop into full bloom. The Rudd government promised boldness but delivered inconsistency. Gillard struggled to cut through in a particularly toxic media environment. Abbott, Turnbull, Morrison each in their own way embodied different aspects of the hollowing out. Vision gave way to tactics. Cabinet government weakened and parties drifted from their bases. Policy became too reactive and institutional memory evaporated almost entirely. Political careers became more about survival than service. The concept of politics as a calling was replaced by the never ending rise of professional political practice.

The bureaucracy, meanwhile, became increasingly sidelined. Consultants and contractors filled the vacuum, often at great cost and with little accountability. As discussed in later chapters, governments outsourced not just services but policy thinking itself. The public service, once a central institution of democratic governance, became just another cog in the machinery of message management. As departments lost expertise, governments lost capacity. The result was predictable: failures of implementation, short-termism, and policy without coherence.

By the 2010s, the hollow state was no longer emergent, it had become entrenched. The symptoms were visible across the political system. Parties had become mere shell organisations, media cycles grew shorter, trust collapsed. The public sensed the emptiness but perhaps expected leaders to lead. The system no longer rewarded long-term thinking or courageous leadership. Instead it rewarded caution, conformity, and the art of saying something while doing nothing. The politicians who succeeded were not those with the strongest convictions or clearest visions, but those best able to navigate 'the game', as the title of Sydney Morning Herald columnist Sean Kelly's book on Scott Morrison conveyed.

That, ultimately, is what defines the hollow state: a political order that retains the rituals of democracy but is stripped of its substance. The buildings still stand, the elections still happen and the machinery still whirs. But what once animated the system: vision, conviction, public service and institutional memory, have all been systematically hollowed out. And the process began not with a crash, but with simple drift. Not with a crisis, but with a series of compromises. Not even with an absence of reform, at least at its early stages, but with the wrong lessons learnt.

Within Australian democracy something deeper is amiss. Something structural and cultural that undermines the substance of democratic governance. This is the paradox at the heart of the hollow state: it persists as an apparatus of authority but is increasingly disconnected from purpose, conviction, or capacity. Power is exercised, often arbitrarily, but to what meaningful end?

This book is about that disjuncture: between appearance and reality, between performance and principle. It traces the steady decline in the quality of Australian public life and examines the institutional and cultural transformations that have contributed to the erosion. What emerges is a portrait of a political system still capable of functioning at a procedural level but bereft of vision, conviction, and trust.
The hollowing out has not been total by any means, but it has been pervasive. It has reshaped politics, government, and public discourse in ways that are corrosive.

The chapters that follow unpack the causes and consequences. Each contributes to the argument of the book: that Australian politics is experiencing a slow-motion crisis — not of collapse, but of emptiness. A loss of conviction, institutional integrity and democratic responsiveness. This is the story of the hollow state.

We begin with an overview of the 2025 federal election, perhaps the least inspiring showdown in modern memory. A government that had underwhelmed during most of its first term in office resoundingly defeated an opposition that failed to articulate a clear alternative agenda beyond one thought bubble big idea. Equally, the campaign itself degenerated into a slanging match, dominated by spin. While Labor won the election convincingly, its mandate lacks bold ideas for reform. The campaign that played out was a perfect illustration of the hollowing out of Australian political discourse.

Chapter 2, *The Managerial Class Takes Over* examines the rise of the political professional. Politics in Australia has become a career path rather than a calling, with candidates often emerging not from communities or movements, but from staffer ranks and lobbying firms. The result is a class of leaders trained in communications without convictions. Individuals selected not for what they believe in but for how they perform. This evolution has reshaped the character of political leadership. Ideological commitment has been displaced by operational competence, or at least the appearance of it. The managerial class governs with an eye on optics, deploying focus-grouped messaging and crisis management techniques in place of genuine policy engagement. This chapter traces how and why this shift occurred, and what it has meant for democratic accountability.

Chapter 3, *The Collapse of Conviction* explores the intellectual shallowness now endemic in Australian politics. Once, political parties anchored themselves in coherent ideologies and policy platforms. Debate was fierce, but it was grounded in ideas. Today, the centre of political gravity has shifted: not to the left or right, but toward emptiness. Electoral survival has replaced ideological debate on all sides. Policy positions are reverse-engineered from polling data. Even when governments act, they often do so without an organising principle, rendering policymaking erratic, inconsistent, or just plain opportunistic. In this chapter, I chart the decline of conviction politics and explain how both major parties have contributed to the ideological vacuum that's followed.

The Triumph of Tactics (Chapter 4) builds on this analysis by focusing on the shift from strategy to short-termism. Winning the 24-hour news cycle has become the primary objective of parties and MPs seeking a leg up. Governments and oppositions operate in permanent campaign mode, prioritising immediate gain over long-term outcomes. Political communication is no longer designed to persuade or inform but to dominate the narrative, often by discrediting opponents rather than defending ideas. This has implications not only for political debate but for the quality of government. Policy coherence suffers as a result. Reform is abandoned in favour of risk management. And voters, subjected to a constant stream of spin and scare campaigns, disengage.

Chapter 5, *The Cult of Personality,* explores how the personalisation of politics has compounded the hollowing out. Leadership has always mattered in democratic systems, but it now dominates to a degree that eclipses party identity, collective responsibility, and long-term policy ambition. Media cycles and political marketing have converged to elevate leaders as brands, reducing complex political agendas to slogans attached to a single personality. This is not merely about popularity contests, it has real consequences for governing. Cabinet decision-making is weakened, dissent is suppressed and entire election campaigns are structured around the image and instincts of one individual leader. In this chapter I examine the rise of presidential-style politics in what is meant to be a Westminster style system, and the ways in which it distorts leadership, accountability and institutional balance.

In *The Great Hollowing Out* (Chapter 6), we turn to the institutions themselves. Parliament, once the centrepiece of meaningful debate and scrutiny, now operates as little more than a stage for partisan performances. The public service, once a reservoir of policy expertise and independent advice, has become politicised and timid. And political parties, once the engine room of citizen engagement and ideological clarity, have become hollow shells, dominated by factional operatives lacking ideological convictions and disconnected from the communities they are supposed to represent. This chapter maps out how these institutional shifts occurred, as well as how weakened parliaments, compromised bureaucracies and hollowed-out parties have accelerated the emergence of a performative, directionless body politic.

Chapter 7, *'Leadership' without Legacy* — investigates the nature of political leadership in the modern era, through the lens of recent prime ministers whose tenures were defined more by their media strategies or tactical cunning than by enduring achievements. In the past, prime ministers left ideological legacies or major reformist imprints. Increasingly, they leave behind little more than a record of political survival, when they even do survive. This chapter evaluates how leadership has become reactive, shaped by polls and crises rather than guided by purpose. The political tail now wags the dog. It also considers the implications of this trend: not only the inability to enact reform, but the loss of any expectation that leaders should aspire to more than the daily grind of political messaging.

Chapter 8, *The Party's Over*, addresses the transformation of political parties from mass-membership institutions into hollowed-out campaign machines. Once rooted in civic participation and ideological contestation, the major parties now operate more like electoral franchises, sustained by professional staffers, donor networks and factional operatives rather than the broader public. Rank-and-file influence has diminished, preselections are often stage-managed, and party conferences have become exercises in symbolism rather than substantive debate. Internal democracy is compromised by a culture of control and fear of dissent. This chapter explores how parties have been drained of their representative and deliberative functions — key pillars of a functioning democracy — and what has been lost as a result.

The erosion of the public service is the focus of Chapter 9. Here we turn to the machinery of government, where expertise has been devalued and independence systematically undermined. As governments have become more focused on perception than outcomes, so too have bureaucrats adapted, shaping advice to suit ministerial expectations or outsourcing responsibility to consultants. The depoliticised professionalism that once characterised the Australian Public Service has given way to something more fragile: a bureaucracy that exists in name but not always in substance. This chapter shows how the decline in bureaucratic independence and capability feeds into the broader themes of hollow governance.

In *The Fourth Estate in Retreat* (Chapter 10) attention turns to the media's role in enabling, amplifying and at times accelerating the hollowing out of Australian politics. The Australian media landscape has undergone significant commercial and technological disruptions, eroding its ability to act as a robust democratic watchdog. At the same time, structural pressures such as shrinking newsrooms, clickbait incentives and the rise of infotainment, have encouraged forms of journalism that prioritise speed, sensationalism and access over scrutiny, context or depth. The consequences are visible daily: more shallow reporting, predictable outrage cycles, and a diminishing capacity to hold power to account. This chapter examines how the press has moved from being a check on politics to a participant in its theatre, and how that has contributed to the hollowing out of Australian politics.

Chapter 11, *Democracy in Decline*, draws the threads together to assess how the patterns traced across previous chapters have impacted citizen engagement and institutional legitimacy. Australia's democratic foundations remain intact on paper, but in practice they have been gradually worn down. Voter turnout is declining even under compulsory voting. Trust in government has collapsed. Engagement with politics is increasingly driven by cynicism, not hope. Where once democracy invited participation and promised progress, now it often feels like a shell game: predictable, scripted and ultimately unsatisfying. This chapter argues that the democratic crisis is not just one of perception, but of substance, When citizens feel their voices don't matter and their votes won't change very much, the health of the system itself comes under threat.

Chapter 12, *Reform Without Courage*, focuses on the retreat from ambition in public policy. For decades, Australia enjoyed a reputation for bold reform: floating the dollar, introducing Medicare, gun control, the GST and more. Many years ago Australia was a world leader in institutional reforms such as compulsory and preferential voting systems. We were also one of the first countries to grant women voting and representative rights. But in recent years, reform has become the political third rail, too risky to touch. Instead of long-term thinking, we see drift and delay. Royal commissions are used as substitutes for action, consultation becomes camouflage for inaction, and white papers gather dust. Institutional reform is almost entirely off the table now. This chapter investigates how political timidity, driven by short-term media cycles, factional instability and fear of backlash, has gutted the will for change. When courage disappears from policymaking, reform does too, and the consequences for the country are profound.

What happens when power is treated as an end in itself? What does it mean for a political system when those in office are more concerned with managing their position than wielding power to improve the nation? Chapter 13 examines the shift from governing to maintaining power, from leadership to incumbency. Policy is too often reactive, cobbled together to manage crises or placate interest groups. Vision is replaced by narrative control. Purpose is hollowed out. This chapter argues that the Australian political class is caught in a cycle of inertia, unable or unwilling to govern with clarity, consistency or courage. Power is retained, but its purpose is lost almost entirely.

The final chapter, *Beyond the Hollow State*, turns outward and forward. It asks what can be done to arrest the decline and restore some of what has been lost. While the book does not pretend to offer a panacea, this chapter offers some fresh ideas: about strengthening institutions, reforming political parties, reviving public service capability and rebuilding trust in the media. It considers whether new forms of citizen engagement or institutional innovation could reverse the trends that have hollowed out Australian democracy. If the hollow state is a product of political, institutional and cultural shifts, then the solution (if there is one) must be equally comprehensive.

I do not pretend that there was a golden age of Australian politics. The system has always had its flaws: entrenched interests, adversarial tendencies and institutional inertia among them. But there was a time when purpose animated politics, when leaders pursued reform agendas with ideological clarity or a sense of national interest, and when institutions retained enough autonomy and capacity to act as stabilising forces. That time has passed.

The Hollow State is, ultimately, a warning. Not a call to nostalgia, but a call to attention. A democracy cannot function indefinitely on the fumes of past legitimacy. It requires constant maintenance: of its norms, its institutions and its expectations of public life. If politics continues to be conducted without conviction, without courage and without purpose, the public will eventually respond in kind: with apathy at best, contempt at worst.

Chapter 1

THE 2025 ELECTION: A HOLLOW CONTEST

Introduction: A Campaign of Echoes

The 2025 federal election should have been a contest of ideas. Instead, it became a hollow ritual, where political engagement was reduced to slogans and strategy. Labor was returned with an increased majority, but without a fresh mandate of any significance or a bold reform agenda. The Coalition failed to offer a compelling alternative, weighed down by an unpopular leader and a policy platform that barely scratched the surface of the nation's challenges.

The campaign reinforced how far Australian politics has drifted from substance. Political parties talked around the big issues: the housing crisis, a strained health system, stagnating productivity, and the need for meaningful climate adaptation. Instead, voters were fed a steady diet of spin, soundbites, and manufactured outrage. For those paying attention, it was hard to miss the vacuum, a campaign driven not by conviction but by political calculations that simply led to more spending coupled with negative attacks.

Labor's message was one of stability, continuity, and risk aversion, a deliberate strategy designed to consolidate, not inspire. The Coalition, led by Peter Dutton, struggled to land meaningful blows. It gestured vaguely at cultural anxieties and economic concerns, but failed to cohere around a policy narrative that cut through. With both major parties running campaigns of avoidance, it's little wonder voter disengagement deepened. Primary support for Labor and the Coalition remained low, ultimately falling to a record low for the Coalition.

This wasn't just an uninspiring election. It was an expression of a broader political malaise: a system hollowed out by years of short-thinking, internal factionalism, and a retreat from policy ambition. What unfolded during the 2025 campaign was a hollow contest, in every sense.

The Opposition's Void

Oppositions don't win elections simply by pointing to government shortcomings, they must offer a clear alternative. At the 2025 election, the Liberal Party failed to do either. Under Peter Dutton's leadership, the Coalition limped through the campaign without a coherent policy vision or a persuasive reason for voters to return them to power after just one term. Their offering was largely a hollow shell, assembled from recycled culture war talking points and vague appeals to cost-of-living anxieties. It was an opposition in name more than in function, reactive, directionless and fundamentally unsure of what it stood for. The one major policy of note — nuclear power — lacked design details and the costings were loose at best.

Dutton entered the campaign burdened by low personal approval ratings and persistent doubts about his electability. Despite some efforts to soften his image in the lead-up to the election, a brief pivot toward "kitchen table issues" and attempts to rebrand as economically competent, these efforts never took root. The electorate saw through the performance.

The Coalition's central economic pitch focused on inflation and interest rates, but offered little that was original or detailed in response. Its centrepiece, a proposal to "remove the roadblocks" to nuclear energy, was emblematic of the broader problem. Promoted heavily by Dutton, the policy had been circulating within the party for years with little development. By 2025, it still lacked modelling, costings, or a timeline, and raised more questions than it answered. That didn't stop the Opposition Leader from touring regional electorates promoting hypothetical sites for future nuclear plants, all while dodging scrutiny about feasibility and public support. The announcement was more about signalling to an anxious electorate and to the party's conservative base that the opposition had an idea, rather than a substantive attempt at addressing the issue of energy reform. To do so would have required details that were never presented.

In other respects, the Opposition's platform was threadbare. On housing, the Coalition criticised Labor's lack of progress but failed to present a credible alternative. Its housing spokesperson's media appearances were marked by vague commitments to "cut red tape" and "incentivise supply," with no legislative blueprint to support these claims. Michael Sukkar (the Opposition's housing spokesperson) ultimately lost his seat. On climate, the party remained hamstrung by internal division. The moderate wing, largely silenced under Dutton, watched as the leader hedged and obfuscated, unwilling to fully endorse net-zero targets or elaborate on how the party would reach them. Dutton ended up losing the election as well as his own seat.

It wasn't only policy that revealed the void. The campaign lacked narrative cohesion. While Dutton toured outer-suburban seats focusing on crime and "cancel culture," Deputy Leader Sussan Ley was dispatched to inner-city electorates speaking about female representation and diversity, as well as what now looks a more personally focussed national tour implicitly canvassing for party room support for post the election, if she needed it. Instead of complementing one another, these efforts clashed, highlighting the party's internal contradictions rather than masking them. It was the by-product of a party that had not resolved its identity crisis since the 2022 defeat, torn between the reactionary impulses of its conservative flank and the electoral reality that Australia, by and large, was drifting toward progressive values.

The result was a campaign that felt backward-looking and brittle. Where John Howard once combined economic credibility with cultural conservatism in a disciplined and electorally effective narrative, Dutton's leadership offered only fragments. He lacked the authority to impose discipline and the imagination to craft a new path forward. Internal briefings during the campaign reflected this. Liberal staffers expressed frustration at a disjointed national message and confusion over strategic targeting. Shadow ministers were rarely seen campaigning side-by-side, a visual metaphor for a party running as disparate individuals rather than a cohesive team.

Voters noticed. In key marginal seats, Liberal candidates struggled to articulate why they should be elected beyond the refrain that "Labor had failed." A weak narrative after just one term — when no first term government has failed to secure re-election since 1931. Some Liberal MPs even avoided Dutton's presence on the campaign trail altogether, wary of his negative impact on local campaigns. These MPs were among the survivors. Post-election analysis confirmed that Dutton's personal unpopularity was a drag on the party's vote in metropolitan seats, the very places the Coalition needs to win back to return to government.

Even in traditional strongholds, the malaise was visible. In Queensland, where Dutton had once been considered an asset, swings toward independents and minor parties suggested a deeper unease. In South Australia and Victoria, the party underperformed. In Western Sydney, once fertile Liberal ground under Morrison, the message failed to resonate. Disconnected from both urban liberals and regional swing voters, the party found itself squeezed on all sides. In the end the Coalition's share of the 150 seat lower house dropped to the mid 40s. An electoral disaster.

Dutton's defenders will argue he was a victim of timing: leading a first-term opposition is always difficult, and internal renewal takes time. But these structural excuses can't mask the fact that the 2025 campaign was a squandered opportunity. The electorate was open to persuasion on key issues: cost-of-living pressures were real, frustration with Labor's inertia on housing and infrastructure was growing. Yet the Coalition couldn't convert those vulnerabilities into momentum, and it certainly didn't present policy alternatives to address such issues.

What the 2025 campaign made clear was that the Coalition had not yet come to terms with its time in opposition. It had neither renewed its intellectual foundations nor developed a strategy to reconnect with the broader public. Instead, it fell back on slogans and culture war detritus, offering criticism in place of policy and hoping Labor would lose the election rather than trying to win it themselves.

This wasn't simply poor campaigning. It was a deeper reflection of the hollow state in action. A party once rooted in philosophical conviction now drifting through opposition with little to offer beyond nostalgia and noise. The 2025 campaign revealed an Opposition unmoored from its own traditions and unprepared for the demands of modern leadership.

Labor's Strategic Minimalism

Labor's 2025 campaign was a masterclass in political restraint. A strategy built not around vision, but around the careful management of risk. If the Coalition's campaign was marked by confusion and absence, Labor's was defined by its deliberate emptiness, combined with purchasing votes with taxpayers' own money. The party didn't so much sell a plan for the future as quietly reassure voters it wouldn't make things worse, beyond the state of the budget. It was a campaign that said very little and almost nothing meaningful, and won comfortably doing so.

Anthony Albanese entered the election as a first-term Prime Minister who had largely governed ineffectively. His approach to leadership had been defined by a steady-as-she-goes pragmatism after the failure of the voice referendum. Unlike his predecessor Scott Morrison, Albanese had kept the spotlight on his ministers, avoided overexposure, and resisted the urge to make grand promises. The 2025 campaign leaned into this minimalist posture, portraying him as a safer pair of hands in a chaotic world than the Liberal Party alternative.

This strategy worked in part because of the vacuum to their right. The Coalition failed to present a credible threat, and Albanese exploited that void by running a tightly controlled, gaffe-free campaign, having learnt from his 2022 go-around. Media appearances were carefully stage-managed. Policy announcements were incremental and framed within existing commitments. Ministers were briefed to stay on message and avoid being drawn into anything resembling a messy debate. The entire campaign resembled a corporate risk register: control the inputs, avoid volatility, win by default against an unpopular opposition leader after just one term in office.

Labor's signature announcement, a modest expansion of its *Future Made in Australia* policy, typified this approach. Marketed as a jobs-and-industry initiative, it allowed the government to talk about economic nationalism without committing to major structural reform. The proposal was safe, largely uncontroversial, and perfectly engineered to sound ambitious while remaining familiar. It let Labor project purpose without provoking scrutiny. The broader campaign never strayed far from this formula. It lacked the necessary underpinnings of tax and federation reforms to add meat to the bones of the policy title.

Where there were vulnerabilities, they were managed rather than tackled. On housing, the government was under pressure. Affordability had worsened, and construction supply chains remained sluggish. Instead of offering bold solutions, Labor promised more of the same: an acceleration of existing schemes, minor tweaks to Commonwealth Rent Assistance, and vague commitments to "unlock supply." All with large injections of spending funded by debt. There was no serious engagement with planning reform, tax incentives, or intergovernmental coordination. But that was the point. Boldness was a liability in a campaign engineered to maintain the status quo.

Even in areas where the government had room to campaign assertively, it chose the path of caution. Climate policy, for instance, had been a centrepiece of the 2022 victory. By 2025, the politics had shifted. Albanese and his team quietly dropped the rhetoric of urgency and pivoted to themes of "practical progress" and "balanced targets." It was a conscious retreat from ambition, designed to avoid a fight with industry, conservative media, or voters wary of perceived overreach. When challenged on emissions targets or the pace of transition, the response was boilerplate: we're meeting our targets, we're creating jobs, we're staying the course. Substance was lacking.

The most striking example of Labor's strategic minimalism was its refusal to engage with the broader policy architecture. No tax reform. No major social policy initiatives. No overhaul of public sector delivery. Education, aged care, and defence were all backgrounded in the campaign, despite simmering concerns in each portfolio. It wasn't that voters didn't care, it was that Labor calculated they didn't care enough to risk shaking the tree. In that sense, the campaign became an exercise in political triage: do only what is necessary, say only what is safe.

Albanese himself was emblematic of the approach. His media appearances were brief and disciplined. Questions were deflected rather than answered, particularly on contentious issues like public sector performance or international trade. His presence on the campaign trail was calibrated to avoid risk: tightly controlled walk-throughs, pulling out his medicare card for the cameras. There were also community roundtables with loyal candidates, and almost no direct debate with the Opposition Leader even in the multiple leaders debates, courtesy of the formats insisted upon. The Prime Minister ran a campaign built on incumbency, not inspiration.

It worked, of course. Labor not only held its ground but expanded its parliamentary majority to a record majority. Yet the victory came at a cost, not to Labor's electoral fortunes, but to the health of political discourse. In a functioning democracy, elections should be moments of engagement, renewal, and debate. The 2025 campaign offered none of that. Labor treated the campaign as a threat to be neutralised, not an opportunity to lead a national conversation to be able to deliver a reforming agenda out the other side in victory.

The strategy also reinforced the broader trend of shrinking political horizons. By choosing not to make the campaign about ideas, Labor effectively signalled that politics is no longer the place for serious problem-solving. It is a competition of competence, not conviction, A management exercise where success is measured by one's ability to avoid risk, not embrace it. That may be good short-term politics, and it works for those seeking a career in parliament and in power. But it corrodes public trust in the long run and achieves little beyond retaining power.

Labor's tactical brilliance lay in its ability to make caution look like leadership, to some extent anyway. But in doing so, it validated the very hollowness this book critiques. The party ran not on a new vision for the country, but on the absence of a credible alternative. It won by being the least hollow vessel on offer, hardly a triumphant endorsement of the health of the political system.

A Vote Without Faith

The 2025 election produced a seemingly decisive result. Labor was returned with an increased majority, consolidating power across marginal and once-contested seats. But beneath the surface of this political triumph sat a deeper paradox: a government winning big without saying much, rewarded for caution rather than ambition.
If elections are meant to deliver a mandate, this one didn't. Not in a substantive sense. It delivered control. Labor's success was less a vote of confidence than a collective shrug, a public going through the motions of democracy without much expectation that it would change anything. Labor's mandate was to do better in its second term because voters weren't interested in the alternative on offer.

Labor's policy offerings were modest even if its spending wasn't. The government's messaging was cautious. Its campaign was engineered to avoid risk and withstand scrutiny rather than inspire or galvanise support. Yet it won very comfortably. Why? Because the alternative, a directionless Coalition led by a deeply unpopular Peter Dutton, was so manifestly uninspiring that many voters defaulted to Labor by necessity, not with conviction. The choice was framed as binary, and in the absence of a credible alternative, voters stuck with the known quantity.

This wasn't a vote of faith in Labor or the job it had done in its first term. It was a vote of fatigue. Labor certainly gained seats, but it didn't gain a mandate for meaningful reform. It avoided hard questions on housing, tax, productivity and climate adaptation. It left aged care, higher education and health system reform in the too-hard basket, even if it threw money at each policy area. Forgiving 20 percent of HECS debts, for example, doesn't even resemble reform to the higher education sector. It is a simple case of buying votes. This is the modern shape of electoral politics in the hollow state: win big by offering little by way of reform but plenty in hand outs.

The electorate's growing scepticism about politics as a forum for serious problem-solving was also reflected in the persistent drift toward minor parties and independents. While the structural dominance of the major parties remained largely intact, particularly in the House of Representatives, a significant portion of voters sought out alternatives, even if those alternatives weren't always successful. The trend was clear: dissatisfaction is rising, but no one is yet capitalising on it. Nobody should mistake occasional electoral failures by minor parties and independents with a growing trend amongst voters to cast their first preference for someone other than the major parties. The 2025 election matched the 2022 results in this respect.

The Greens, often positioned as the natural leftward alternative, retained their all important senate positions, giving them the balance of power in the second chamber. Yet the Greens' lower house ambitions stalled. The loss of leader Adam Bandt's seat of Melbourne fed a media narrative of decline that wasn't borne out in the data. The Greens vote in overall terms remained high. Still, lower house failures underscored the limitations of a party still struggling to bridge the gap between protest politics and national relevance.

The Teal independents, who reshaped the 2022 election by toppling prominent Liberals in affluent inner-city seats, found the terrain a little tougher this time. The conditions had shifted. Without the Morrison-era scandals or the same sense of urgency around integrity and climate, the Teals' campaigns felt more diffuse. Albanese had absorbed elements of their agenda, and Dutton's opposition while reactionary, wasn't a governing target in the way Morrison had been. As a result, the electoral momentum simply wasn't there. Zoe Daniel lost her seat of Goldstein and Monique Ryan came close to losing Kooyong.

That didn't stop these candidates from performing well in the broader context of how difficult it is for independents to win lower house seats. In many electorates, they forced major parties to divert resources, shift messaging, and moderating policy positions. But the real significance of their performance wasn't in seats gained or lost, it was in what their continued presence revealed. The Liberal Party remains weak in its traditional heartland, and a growing swathe of the electorate remains unconvinced by either side of politics.

All of this points to a political system under strain. The major parties remain institutionally dominant but ideologically hollow. The minor parties and independents attract attention but often lack the reach, consistency, or infrastructure to pose a serious alternative. Voters cycle between disengagement and tactical re-engagement, not because they believe in the process, but because they are trying to minimise damage. What looks like stability from the outside is, in fact, stasis: a democracy functioning procedurally but eroding in meaning.

The 2025 election wasn't a moment of renewal. It wasn't a realignment either. It wasn't even a contest of competing futures. It was, in almost every respect, a placeholder election. A choice between parties that offered little, where the party that offered less risk won by default, especially in the international context of a returning Donald Trump presidency. Labor's large majority did not reflect an enthusiastic public endorsement. It reflected the absence of a credible alternative.

That is the defining feature of the hollow state. A political culture in which elections are no longer about persuasion or principle, but about management. Where parties fight over control, not direction. Where voters participate, but no longer invest. In 2025, the system delivered a winner, but it didn't deliver much of a mandate and it certainly didn't deliver purpose.

Media Without Memory

If the 2025 election campaign exposed the strategic emptiness of the major parties, it also laid bare the failings of the media tasked with holding them to account. Across print, broadcast and digital platforms, the coverage was as hollow as the politics it reported on. Instead of interrogating policy vacuums, journalists obsessed over daily tactics. Instead of spotlighting contradictions, they amplified distractions. The campaign wasn't just stage-managed by political operatives, it was cheerfully enabled by a press gallery that has forgotten how to report politics as a contest of ideas.

The dominant mode of coverage was horse-race journalism, a breathless fixation on polls, optics and message discipline. Each morning brought new campaign trail visuals and vox pops. Each evening closed with commentary panels speculating on swings in outer-suburban marginals. But nowhere in that cycle was there serious scrutiny of what was missing: a debate about the country's direction, the institutional decay eroding service delivery, or the policy failures compounding housing unaffordability. The media reflected the spectacle without ever questioning its emptiness.

Leaders' debates, once an opportunity for the press to press, became just another performance. Questions focused on trivia or manufactured gaffes. Policy contradictions were allowed to stand unchallenged. When Albanese was pressed, it was rarely on his government's lack of ambition. When Dutton was tested, it was typically on tone rather than substance. Journalists repeatedly let both leaders off the hook. The fourth estate didn't forget how to ask hard questions, it forgot why they matter.

Perhaps the most telling media failure was the treatment of minor parties and independents. The Teals and Greens received saturation coverage, far more than their seat share warranted, but were rarely subjected to serious policy scrutiny. Teal candidates were profiled as local heroes, community favourites, disruptors of the status quo. But few were pressed on economic literacy, legislative agendas or how they would wield influence if elected. The Greens, meanwhile, were reduced to caricature, presented either as an inner-city conscience or an obstacle to pragmatism, depending on the outlet.

The media fixation on Adam Bandt's defeat in Melbourne was a case in point. His loss became a dominant narrative in post-election coverage, held up as evidence of the Greens' electoral limits. But there was little effort to contextualise it: the fact that the party's national vote remained stable or that it retained key senate spots or that electoral boundaries shifted not in Bandt's favour. Complexity gave way to storyline infotainment. The loss became "the story" even if the data didn't support the takeout.

This tendency to focus on narrative over nuance wasn't new, but it was particularly corrosive in a campaign already starved of substance. The media's obsession with "momentum" and "game-changers" ensured that policies that didn't create immediate conflict were ignored. Labor's thin housing package wasn't unpicked. The Coalition's uncosted nuclear plan was never seriously interrogated. The near-total silence on tax reform, public sector reform or aged care challenges went, for the most part, unremarked upon. In a healthier democracy, these absences would be news. In 2025, they barely registered.

Social media, once thought to democratise the political conversation, only made matters worse. Campaign content was repackaged into digestible soundbites, curated for engagement rather than insight. Viral moments: a candidate's stumble, a debate zinger, a campaign ad blunder, drove coverage cycles. Parties leaned into the algorithmic logic, crafting messaging designed to generate reactions rather than inform. Labor just did it better. The press followed suit, amplifying clicks over clarity. This wasn't a glitch in the system, it was the system functioning exactly as it's now built.

The role of the major mastheads further reflected the hollowness of the media environment. *The Australian* remained wedded to its ideological campaigns, framing the election as a cultural contest between conservative values and progressive overreach. *The Sydney Morning Herald* and *The Age*, once standard-bearers of liberal centrist analysis, veered toward soft profiles and access journalism. The ABC, under constant political pressure and internal caution, avoided provocation altogether, other than its inherent left wing bias amongst high profile commentators and journalists. The result was a political media that spoke often, but said little of value.

None of this is to deny that some excellent journalism still occurred. A handful of journalists pursued real scrutiny of housing policy, climate and energy frameworks, and productivity reform. But these were exceptions, and they were rarely front-page priorities. The broader media culture remained locked in a loop: report what's said, not what's avoided. Follow the spectacle, not the substance.

In that context, it's little wonder voters disengaged. If the media treats politics as theatre, the audience will eventually tune out. Trust in politicians and the press alike remained low. The public saw a campaign filled with images, messaging, and branding but with no argument, no purpose, and no shared understanding of what the election was meant to decide.

The media didn't create the hollow state but it reflected it. And in doing so, it deepened the malaise. In a political system already drained of vision, a press gallery that rewards strategy over substance becomes an accomplice. The 2025 election wasn't just a missed opportunity for political leadership. It was a missed opportunity for journalism, the kind that holds the powerful to account, demands clarity and insists that elections be more than managed performances.

The fourth estate remains vital to democratic health, but in 2025 it did not rise to that task. It mirrored the hollowness it should have challenged, and the result was a campaign remembered for what it avoided, not what it addressed.

An Election Without a Mandate?

The 2025 federal election delivered Labor a larger parliamentary majority, a weaker Coalition opposition, and a legislature that looks deceptively stable. But what it did not deliver, to any party or political movement, was a meaningful mandate. Not for reform, not for renewal, not even for clarity. This was not an election won with vision or lost through the contest of ideas. It was won because one side made fewer mistakes than the other, and lost because the alternative failed to articulate a reason to exist, falling victim to the unpopularity of its leader. What remained at the end was a government with power, but little purpose. A political class returned to office, but with no sense of direction.

In a functioning democracy, an election result of this magnitude would usually spark a period of policy ambition. Big majorities usually bring with them big expectations. Yet the 2025 result has instead produced more drift. Even on election night when the numbers revealed the size of Labor's victory, the Treasurer sitting on the ABC's coverage ruled out using the win to institute meaningful reforms not flagged during the hollow campaign. Labor, emboldened by numbers but constrained by its own caution, has signalled no significant departure from its pre-election posture. Its victory has been interpreted not as a call for reform but as vindication of its incrementalism. The message taken from the campaign was that doing less works so why do more?

That logic sits at the heart of the hollow state. Elections continue, parties campaign, governments form, but the substantive content of politics is reduced to tactics, positioning and risk management. The 2025 contest confirmed this dynamic. Labor's strategists read the electorate accurately: the public was risk-averse, disengaged, and wary of overreach. Their campaign was built around those assumptions. It succeeded electorally, but at the cost of reinforcing a dangerous precedent: that political success no longer depends on policy ambition or ideological clarity, only on surviving the cycle.

The Coalition's performance compounded the problem. A party that once prided itself on being the standard-bearer of economic management and centre-right conviction now limped through the campaign with cultural scraps and fragmented messaging. It did not lose because it was attacked, it lost because it offered nothing by way of an alternative. Post-election, the party so far has offered little in the way of introspection. There was no coherent diagnosis of failure, no clear plan for renewal, and no serious conversation about its disconnection from the progressive drift of mainstream Australia.

The political system is visibly failing to inspire or deliver, yet it continues largely unchallenged. There is enough institutional gravity to keep the major parties afloat. Enough residual loyalty — in the regions, generationally and ideologically — to prop up legacy brands. Enough fear of the alternative to keep voters returning to parties they no longer particularly trust. But there is no energy, no new consensus, no shared ambition for what the nation might become. Instead, there is just management, and not very good management at that. The administration of government by politicians who increasingly define their success by what they avoid.

This is not sustainable. Politics without purpose corrodes democratic legitimacy. When governments take power without a clear agenda, and when oppositions contest power without one, the public rightly tunes out. Civic trust erodes. Reform becomes harder. Short-termism becomes the default. Institutions hollow out, and elections become pageants: expensive, performative, and disconnected from the challenges they are supposed to address.

The 2025 campaign should have been an opportunity. Australia faced real, urgent issues: a housing crisis worsening by the month, a climate transition still mired in incrementalism, a health system buckling under demand, an ageing population, declining productivity and growing geopolitical complexity. None of these problems can be solved by electoral calculus. They require leadership, vision and meaningful public debate. Yet the 2025 election campaign offered none of that. The silence on these fronts wasn't accidental, it was strategic. And that silence was reinforced, not challenged, by the media, the parties and the public. A triumvirate of failure by all participants in the democratic polity.

In that context, the size of Labor's win became less impressive than it first appeared. It wasn't an endorsement of a plan, it was the absence of an alternative. The government now holds a large majority, but without a clear sense of what that majority is for. It commands a Parliament with the capacity to act, but no real pressure to do so. This disconnect, between institutional power and political ambition, is the clearest marker of the hollow state in action.

What remains is a political system in stasis. Government continues while the opposition reshuffles. Media resumes its cycle, but none of it carries much weight. The political class operates within a closed loop responsive only to itself, congratulating itself on tactics while the public grows more distant and disillusioned. It is a system performing the rituals of democracy without the content that really matters.

The 2025 election did not break this pattern, it confirmed it and reenforced it. It will be remembered not for any defining issue, transformative moment or reimagined mandate, but for how little really changed. And that, more than any policy or seat count, tells us what kind of state we are now living in. It's a hollow one.

Chapter 2
THE MANAGERIAL CLASS TAKES OVER

Introduction

Australian politics has become a contest of personalities, not principles. The ideological anchors that once defined the major parties have been loosened, if not completely severed, leaving behind a political class more focused on electoral tactics than policy outcomes. What was once a battle of ideas has devolved into a marketing exercise: campaigns crafted by consultants, driven by polling, and dominated by spin. Leadership is no longer about conviction, it's about survival. This is not merely a matter of political style, it speaks to a deeper structural failure of the system itself.

Across the last two decades, both major parties have steadily hollowed out. Internal democracy has eroded. Parliamentary candidates are preselected not for their intellectual or ideological contribution, but for their loyalty, media performance and perhaps most significantly their factional alignment. Cabinet and shadow cabinet decisions are increasingly shaped by political operatives rather than elected officials. The result is a culture where conviction is discouraged, complexity is avoided and authenticity is usually punished.

This chapter traces the roots and consequences of this decline. It begins with the rise of focus-group politics, charts the professionalisation of political careers, examines the centralisation of party power and critiques the short-termism that now dominates policy-making. If politics is to recover its sense of purpose it must rediscover the value of having convictions. I'm not talking about nostalgia for ideology's sake, but a return to politics grounded in principle, courage and long-term thinking.

The Era of Managerialism

The shift in Australian politics from conviction-based leadership to managerialism represents one of the most profound changes in the character of governance in recent decades. Where once political leaders were guided by a coherent ideological worldview or deep-seated policy convictions, contemporary political figures increasingly approach their roles through the lens of management theory, focus group feedback and electoral calculus. The language of leadership has been replaced by the vocabulary of messaging, strategy and brand maintenance. The result is a political class more focused on managing perceptions than pursuing a defined policy agenda. Marketing is now the name of the game.

This managerial style of politics is not confined to one side of the ideological spectrum. It is visible across both major parties, although it manifests differently depending on the personalities and power structures involved. In the Labor Party, for instance, we have seen a succession of leaders whose commitment to core Labor principles has been sacrificed on the altar of electability. Kevin Rudd's technocratic style, Julia Gillard's transactional pragmatism and Anthony Albanese's cautious centrism all reflect the turn away from strong, values-driven leadership. On the Coalition side, the trend is arguably even more entrenched. Scott Morrison famously styled himself as a "marketing guy" and governed accordingly: reactive, opportunistic and obsessed with controlling the media narrative. His "daggy dad" persona was a conscious branding exercise, devoid of substantive political meaning.

Managerialism is, at its core, the reduction of politics to mere process. It reflects an assumption that the business of governing can be handled through systems optimisation, stakeholder engagement, and the management of risk. Concepts borrowed from the corporate world. The managerial politician doesn't lead by principle but from a spreadsheet. Ideas become policies only after they've been costed, polled and focus group tested in marginal seats. The result is a bland form of politics that is risk-averse, ideologically shallow and lacking the kind of vision that once animated national debates.

There is, of course, a practical rationale behind the shift. The modern media environment rewards message discipline and punishes deviation from the script. In such a climate, authenticity becomes a liability. Leaders are expected to be "on-message" at all times, wary of providing a soundbite that might derail the day's narrative. Political staffers have become not just advisers but gatekeepers and enforcers of brand protection. As a result, leadership has been hollowed out. Vision is now treated as a threat to stability rather than a sign of political courage.

But this obsession with managing the short-term news cycle comes at a long-term cost. Voters can sense when leaders are merely managing, rather than leading. The erosion of trust in politics is inextricably linked to the perception that politicians say one thing and do another. Not necessarily because they are duplicitous, but because they are constantly recalibrating their message in response to political research (polling and focus groups). They govern with their eyes fixed not on history, but on the next published Newspoll.

Nowhere was this clearer than in the Liberal Party's post-Howard years. After losing office in 2007, the party fell into a period of strategic disorientation, lacking a unifying policy vision. Brendan Nelson, Malcolm Turnbull, and Tony Abbott all led the party within a short span. Each offering a different managerial strategy rather than a clear ideological direction. Even Abbott, who won the 2013 election on a platform displaying some resolve and directness, quickly reverted to micro-political management once he was in power. Abbott's leadership collapsed not because of deep ideological clashes but because of a perception, particularly among his colleagues, that he could not manage the optics and process of governing effectively. He was defeated by the superficial.

The rise of managerialism is not merely a political choice, it is also structural. The professionalisation of politics has created a class of party operatives and politicians whose formative experiences are in political offices, think tanks or lobbying firms. These are not individuals who came into politics with a clear ideological mission or experience running their own businesses, but rather with skills in communications, negotiation and campaign strategy. Their success is measured not by long-term policy impact, but by short-term wins: winning the 24-hour news cycle, surviving preselection and appeasing internal party factions. Conviction, according to this model, is a dangerous indulgence.

Media fragmentation has exacerbated the problem. In a more centralised media age, politicians could afford to pursue controversial or difficult policies, because they had more time and space to explain their rationale. Today, the rush to react, spin and neutralise a political threat leaves little room for long-form argument. Managerial politics fits this environment perfectly. It is designed not to persuade, but to neutralise.

The shift also reflects a loss of internal party democracy. When parties are no longer driven by vibrant grassroots membership and robust debate, but by factional brokers and backroom dealmakers, the space for ideological renewal contracts. The leader becomes a CEO, not a political visionary. And like many CEOs, their main job becomes keeping shareholders (in this case, factions and donors) happy while avoiding reputational risk. Winning elections is a big part of that, political ideology not so much. Policies that appeal to special interests matter, policies that appeal to national wellbeing less so.

Managerialism is not a stable solution to democratic fatigue, it is a symptom of it. A democracy run by managers instead of leaders is one that is slowly eroding the moral authority of politics itself. The more politics resembles a corporate boardroom, the less legitimacy it commands from the public. People do not vote for process, they vote for purpose.

Polling, Focus Groups and the Death of Principle

The reliance on polling and focus groups has become a structural feature of modern politics, but its most corrosive effect is philosophical, It has replaced principle with popularity. Political parties, once grounded in ideological conviction and policy ambition, now operate like consumer brands, testing every move against what the public might tolerate rather than what the country might need. The consequence is not just political blandness, it is the hollowing out of leadership itself.

Where polling was once a tool to supplement political instinct, it has now become the substitute for it. Leaders no longer test public opinion to inform the presentation of policy, they test it to decide whether a policy should exist at all. This inversion of purpose turns the idea of representative democracy on its head. Politicians are meant to lead public opinion, not merely echo it. Edmund Burke promoted this notion of trustee representation. The promise of conviction is that it can persuade people there is a better future. The practice of polling ensures that such ambition never gets off the ground.

The Australian political class is particularly vulnerable to this dynamic. Unlike in presidential systems where individual leaders can cultivate a personal mandate, Australia's party-centric parliamentary structure incentivises risk aversion. When leadership spills can occur overnight, conviction becomes a liability. Why stake your political capital on a controversial policy when your colleagues might knife you for a dip in Newspoll? This creates a perverse incentive structure: leaders are punished not for failure of vision, but for deviation from the safe middle ground.

The Rudd–Gillard–Rudd years were emblematic of this phenomenon. Kevin Rudd's initial popularity was driven not by any core belief system but by his ability to reflect the public mood. When he did try to take on difficult reforms, like climate change, he lost his nerve the moment polling turned against him. Julia Gillard, by contrast, tried to build consensus around difficult decisions like the carbon tax, only to be punished for breaking a pre-election promise. Both leaders ultimately found themselves caught between the politics of polling and the demands of principle. Neither survived.

It is not that polling is inherently corrupting, rather its role has been allowed to expand unchecked. The more parties use focus groups to craft slogans, test policy language and narrowcast their messaging, the more politics becomes a performance rather than a project. Political communication is reduced to its lowest common denominator. Nuance, detail and ideological coherence are treated as risks. What remains is just the shell of politics: press releases, announcements and reactive commentary. There is no oxygen left for actual leadership.

In this environment, the rise of the "small target" strategy has become the default. Opposition parties, in particular, are increasingly unwilling to outline comprehensive policies for fear they will become electoral vulnerabilities. Bill Shorten's 2019 election platform was criticised for daring to offer detail built around an ideological vision. By contrast, Anthony Albanese's 2022 strategy — deliberately vague, cautious and poll-tested — succeeded because it avoided risk.

The lesson absorbed by party strategists was clear: convictions are dangerous.

There is a deeper cultural shift at play too. Voters have become conditioned to expect caution. Political journalism punishes "gaffes" with disproportionate attention, reinforcing the pressure on leaders to stay within tight rhetorical lanes. The ideal political communicator in this context is not a visionary but a tactician. Someone who can survive, not someone who can inspire. The likes of Bob Hawke or Paul Keating never would have succeeded in such an environment. When journalists treat policy inconsistency as more newsworthy than policy inaction, politicians will naturally err on the side of paralysis.

The tragedy is that polling was never designed to lead. It is descriptive, not normative. It tells us what people think in a given moment, not what they might support if presented with a compelling case. Yet political operatives now use polling as a form of vetting: If the public isn't already on board, the idea doesn't make it to the table. This short-circuits democratic leadership at its most basic level. It is the antithesis of persuasion. Leaders become followers of the electorate, not representatives of their best interests.

This phenomenon has also shifted the internal culture of political parties. Rather than being shaped by policy thinkers or ideological debates at the grassroots, strategy is now centralised among a small cadre of campaign professionals and data analysts. These operatives are skilled at winning elections but often lack a substantive vision for governance. Their success is measured not by long-term outcomes but by movement in the fortnightly polls. The result is a political apparatus obsessed with optics, reactive to headlines, and allergic to depth.

Some of the blame lies with the media environment itself. The demand for constant content has intensified pressure on politicians to produce immediate reactions rather than thoughtful responses. Policy development is a slow and often thankless task. Messaging, by contrast, can be crafted overnight and gives egos airtime. Under such conditions, conviction is not just inconvenient, it is structurally discouraged.

The consequence for Australian democracy is a growing disillusionment among voters. When policies appear to be constructed solely for electoral advantage, people rightly question the authenticity of those proposing them. Trust erodes and cynicism grows. Voter disengagement increases and ironically the very polling that guides political behaviour begins to reflect the consequences of that behaviour. It's a feedback loop causing decline.

In this context, it's worth asking what would it take to reverse the damage? The answer is not to abandon polling altogether, but to reassert the primacy of political leadership over political management. Leaders must use polling to inform, not dictate. They must be willing to lose small battles in order to win larger arguments. And most importantly, they must remember that the public often respects courage, even when it disagrees with the specifics. The reward for John Howard's pursuit of the GST ahead of the 1998 election is a perfect example. Voters know when they're being patronised.

The death of principle is not inevitable, but resuscitating it will require a new kind of political courage. One that accepts short-term pain in pursuit of long-term gain. In an era where polling dominates strategy and messaging, such courage is all too rare. But it is precisely what Australian politics needs if it is to recover its purpose.

The Professionalisation of Politics

The career trajectory of the modern politician has become increasingly linear: university politics, an internship or role as a political staffer, a brief stint in a party-affiliated think tank or union and then preselection into a safe seat (or a marginal one if their options are limited). At no point does this pipeline require real-world experience beyond the political bubble. What was once an exception has become the rule. Politics is no longer a vocation for those with a lifetime of expertise or lived experience, it is a career in and of itself, often pursued by individuals who have never stepped outside the machinery of political operations. I have watched and tracked this narrowing of pre-parliamentary backgrounds during my academic career, as have colleagues such as Wayne Errington (now an Associate Professor at Adelaide University).

The professionalisation of politics has led to a monoculture within Parliament House. When MPs and Senators are drawn almost exclusively from political backgrounds, the diversity of experience that once shaped debate and policy formation is lost. Teachers, small business owners, farmers, academics, lawyers and public servants used to populate the parliamentary benches more than they do today. Now, they are the minority, or those spruiking such qualifications and experience are overselling their credentials. Parliament is actually filled with former staffers and party operatives whose expertise lies in managing news cycles, controlling internal party dynamics, and neutralising threats to their own advancement. There has always been a place for such operatives, but they are now too dominant.

This is not just a problem of optics, it is a problem of competence. When politics becomes a closed loop, insulated from the public it purports to represent, the quality of governance suffers. Complex policy problems are reduced to simplistic messaging. Structural reforms are avoided because they are difficult to explain and easy to oppose. The people making the decisions often lack the depth of knowledge to craft bold solutions, relying instead on briefings from their own media advisors or departmental talking points.

The motivations of professional politicians also differ from those who enter politics later in life. A person with a background in business or community advocacy may view political office as a chance to apply their knowledge to the public good. A career politician, by contrast, is often more focused on the next rung of the ladder: ministerial promotion, factional favour or developing a media profile. This breeds a culture of political risk aversion. Why take a principled stand that could cost you support when you've spent your entire adult life (and perhaps part of your youth) positioning for power?

This dynamic hollows out political parties from within. Preselection contests are no longer fought on the basis of merit or ideological distinction but factional loyalty and backroom alliances. Candidates are parachuted into electorates with no local ties, justified by their campaign experience or loyalty to party figures. Once elected they are expected to vote according to the party line, regardless of what their constituents may believe or what they themselves think, if they ever really do. Internal dissent is punished, not debated. The party room becomes an echo chamber, not a forum for genuine exchange.

The Labor Party's factional system institutionalises this dynamic, but the Coalition is not immune. Increasingly, Liberal and National Party candidates are drawn from the same professionalised pool: former ministerial staff, think tank employees, or legal operatives with close ties to factional powerbrokers. The same people advising on campaign strategy often end up as MPs themselves, perpetuating the cycle of political insularity.

The machinery around politicians has evolved in tandem. Where once a local MP might have two or three staff focused on constituent services and policy development, now they have media advisors, digital communications strategists and electorate officers tasked with building their personal brand. Parliamentary work is increasingly shaped by communications imperatives. Press releases are crafted before policies are even finalised. In fact many policies are crafted with the look of the press release front of mind. Social media engagement takes precedence over community consultation. Even policy speeches are often drafted with the primary aim of generating a few favourable headlines, rather than laying out a long-term vision. How they are strategically leaked is the first order of business.

There is also a generational shift to contend with. The traditional path into politics, marked by career experience and community leadership, has been replaced by political apprenticeships. Young operatives move from university student politics straight into political offices, often climbing the ranks without any meaningful experience outside the Canberra bubble. Their loyalty is to the party machine, not to public service. They speak fluently in the language of tactics but often lack grounding in policy detail or economic literacy.

This culture has broader consequences for governance. With fewer MPs and Senators bringing independent expertise to bear on legislative debates, parliamentary committees become rubber stamps, or mere platforms for grandstanding. Policy formulation is outsourced to consultants or interest groups. Ministers are expected to front media appearances with little more than talking points, rather than detailed knowledge of their portfolios. Departmental advice, while still critical, is increasingly filtered through political lenses. The result is a political culture that prizes message discipline over substance and optics over outcomes.

There are, of course, exceptions. Individuals who have broken the mould or brought genuine experience into the political arena. But they are increasingly rare and often treated as outsiders by their own parties. Independent MPs have, in some cases, filled the vacuum, offering a more grounded and policy-driven approach. But within the major parties, the dominance of professional politicians is now so entrenched that it is difficult to see how the trend might be reversed without significant structural reform.

The professionalisation of politics also exacerbates the decline of conviction. When political careers are carefully managed from day one, taking a strong stance on a divisive issue becomes risky. Ambition encourages conformity. Innovation is discouraged. Politicians learn early that their future prospects depend less on the quality of their ideas than on their ability to avoid controversy. The consequences are visible right across the spectrum: timid policies, short-term planning and a lack of vision in both government and opposition.

In many ways, the political class is simply responding to the incentives they face. The media cycle punishes complexity, internal party rules reward loyalty, preselection battles are fought by numbers not ideas. Voters too have come to expect less of their representatives. But none of this excuses the abandonment of leadership. If anything it demands more of those within the system. It requires politicians to resist the gravitational pull of professionalisation and reconnect with the communities they serve. Not just through media stunts, but through genuine policy engagement and public service.

Without a change in who we recruit into politics (and how we prepare them for leadership) the system will continue to decay. Professionalisation may have made campaigns more efficient, but it has left democracy much poorer. Until political parties once again value diversity of experience, independence of thought, and policy expertise — the same way they increasingly value the trinket of diversity optically — the idea of having convictions will remain an endangered species in Australian public life.

Hollow Parties, Hollow Politics

The major political parties in Australia have become mere husks of their former selves: organisationally depleted, ideologically inconsistent and structurally resistant to reform. Once mass membership vehicles for civic participation and policy debate, they are now tightly controlled machines serving narrow interests and careerist objectives. The hollowing out of party institutions has undermined their ability to represent broad constituencies, it has weakened internal democracy and it has contributed directly to the rise of public cynicism and political disengagement.

This is not a problem unique to Australia, but its effects here are acute. Both the Liberal and Labor parties have witnessed dramatic declines in membership over the past few decades. All part of the transition from mass membership parties into electoral professional organisations along the lines political scientist have canvassed. While precise numbers are closely guarded, estimates suggest the combined membership of both major parties may be lower today than at any time since World War II. What remains is a cohort of factionally aligned activists, former staffers and insiders who wield oversized influence in preselections, internal ballots and policy formation (when it happens). The average Australian voter has virtually no pathway into meaningful engagement with party processes these days.

This erosion of membership undermines the claim that parties are representative vehicles of the public will. It also empowers factional elites. Internal contests are no longer genuine expressions of democratic input, but rather orchestrated outcomes negotiated by powerbrokers. Preselection processes are manipulated to install compliant candidates. Dissent is punished through branch stacking or administrative intervention. The broader public is alienated from these opaque, insider-dominated mechanisms, feeding a sense of political illegitimacy and disconnection.

The policy consequences are also clear. When political parties are hollowed out, their platforms become thin, reactive and hostage to the whims of polling and media cycles. Without robust internal deliberation or meaningful grassroots input, party policy risks becoming a tool of electoral strategy rather than a reflection of deeply held values or long-term vision. Even the act of platform development has become performative, driven more by PR imperatives than by genuine ideological or intellectual investment.

In the case of the Liberal Party, this hollowness manifests in a persistent tension between economic liberalism and cultural conservatism, an unresolved ideological fault line that once generated constructive tension but now risks collapse. The party's core identity is increasingly shaped not by philosophical conviction but by whatever message will hold everyone together until the next election. This has produced a political style defined more by what it opposes than what it believes in. Culture war skirmishes replace substantive debate. Economic orthodoxy is abandoned when inconvenient. The party becomes a vehicle for power, not principle.

Labor is locked in the same structural malaise as conservatives. Its factions are institutionalised and frequently prioritise factional advancement over party renewal. The union movement, once a source of policy ballast and social purpose, now operates as a gatekeeper to power rather than a source of grassroots mobilisation. Unions are no longer broadly representative of the working class population. In both major parties, parliamentary wings dominate organisational wings, leaving little room for bottom-up accountability or innovation. Conferences that once debated policy now rubber-stamp decisions made long before delegates arrived.

This state of hollow politics makes parties more vulnerable to external pressure, whether from donors, lobbyists, or consultants. When parties no longer draw their strength from active memberships and internal debate, they compensate by outsourcing thinking and strategy. Consultants pitch policies based on what will cut through. Donors receive privileged access. Lobbyists move seamlessly between ministerial offices and corporate boardrooms. The professionalisation of politics intersects with this hollowness to create a system that is both insular and too easy to manipulate.

At the same time political parties have increasingly relied on transactional relationships with voters. Electoral strategies are built around micro-targeting, fear campaigns and short-term incentives. Long-term policy development takes a back seat to the weekly news cycle. Voters, treated as consumers rather than participants, respond accordingly, detaching from parties and treating political engagement as a cynical exercise. The rise of minor parties and independents is both a symptom of this hollowing out and a response to it.

There was a time when joining a political party was an act of civic engagement. It offered a forum for debate, a chance to shape the direction of the country and a way to influence candidate selection. Today, the parties have little interest in such engagements. Many preselection battles are resolved through backroom deals or controlled by factional warlords. Members are often treated as liabilities, likely to introduce conflict, slow down decisions or challenge authority. This inversion of the democratic ideal weakens the parties from within and degrades their capacity to govern with legitimacy.

Rebuilding party vitality requires more than structural tinkering. It demands cultural change. Parties must once again value internal diversity, ideological contestation and grassroots empowerment. That means loosening the grip of factions, opening up preselection processes, and investing in civic education and political participation. It also means resisting the temptation to centralise power in the leader's office, a trend that has increasingly replaced party forums with personal fiefdoms.

Such change won't be easy. The incentives all point the other way: Leaders want control, factions want stability, campaign managers want message discipline. But the long-term cost of hollow parties is a hollow democracy. If political institutions are to regain public trust, they must begin by restoring internal legitimacy. That requires courage, transparency and a willingness to cede power back to the membership. Until that happens, Australia's major parties will remain weak vehicles for real political leadership, and voters will continue to look elsewhere for representation.

The Cult of Leadership

Australian politics has become increasingly presidential in nature, with party leaders elevated above the teams they lead and even above the institutions they represent. The shift from party-centred to leader-centred politics has transformed the dynamics of policy-making, campaign strategy and public accountability. Leadership has always mattered, but the contemporary obsession with personality over process has weakened collective governance and elevated style above substance.

Leaders are now marketed like brands: packaged, promoted and protected through professionalised political operations. The modern leader is expected to be across everything, the face of every policy, the centre of every announcement. This creates a distorted sense of political power, where success or failure is attributed almost exclusively to the individual at the top, regardless of the underlying realities of governance or the collaborative nature of parliamentary systems. The consequence is a politics of centralisation, where prime ministers and opposition leaders dominate their parties and shape their identities in ways that would have been unthinkable a generation ago.

Part of this phenomenon is driven by media logic. The 24-hour news cycle demands constant content, and leaders are the most recognisable source. The press gallery focuses on the top of the ticket, often reducing political coverage to personality analysis and leadership speculation. Polling companies, in turn, reinforce this dynamic by measuring preferred prime minister ratings and leader satisfaction scores, metrics that are increasingly treated as proxies for electoral viability. Campaigns reflect this narrow focus: the leader's tour dominates the schedule, while other candidates are relegated to the margins.

But the cult of leadership is not just a product of media or polling. It reflects deeper shifts within the political parties themselves. Parliamentary caucuses and party memberships have been systematically sidelined in favour of tighter control by the leader's office. In many cases, leaders now wield greater influence over preselection, policy formulation and campaign decisions than their predecessors ever did. Shadow cabinets and cabinets alike are often little more than formalities, rubber-stamping decisions made elsewhere. So-called kitchen cabinets now dominate: inner circles within the formal inner circles of government.

Rather than confronting structural problems or reassessing ideological direction, parties often seek quick fixes through leadership changes. The idea that a change at the top can resolve fundamental issues has led to a revolving-door culture that prioritises optics over substance. After the stability of the Howard years, since 2007 Australia has had a rapid succession of prime ministers, some elected, others deposed by their own colleagues. This churn has not just been destabilising; it has eroded the public's faith in political stability and deepened cynicism about political motives.

Leadership spills have become political events in and of themselves, staged with the theatre of high-stakes drama but often lacking any genuine policy rationale. I know because during my time working on

Sky News I saw how they unfold directly. In too many cases, leadership contests are driven by internal polling, media momentum or factional calculation, not ideological divergence or national interest. This trend has only intensified the disconnect between parties and the public. Voters are left to wonder who is really in control, and why leaders are changed without electoral input. Fortunately this revolving door seems to have temporarily stopped, but perhaps only for a time.

This over-reliance on changes of leadership as the solution to all political problems diminishes the role of ideas, institutions and collective governance. Leaders become scapegoats for failure and lightning rods for discontent. But they are also afforded unchecked authority while in office, precisely because they are seen as central to electoral success. The result is a political culture that lacks stability and depth. It encourages short-term thinking, suppresses internal dissent and weakens the role of ministers and backbenchers alike.

In the Liberal Party, this dynamic has been particularly pronounced. Leadership changes from Turnbull to Morrison to Dutton have occurred against the backdrop of ideological drift and factional pressure. Rather than settling debates about the party's direction, these transitions have often exacerbated internal divisions. The decision to remove Turnbull, for instance, was not about competence or electoral performance, it was about ideological control. Yet his successor, Morrison, largely governed with pragmatism rather than principle, further muddying the waters of what the party stands for.

Labor, too, has not been immune. The Rudd-Gillard-Rudd saga left lasting damage to the party's credibility and highlighted the internal power struggles that now characterise leadership politics when it sets in. Even when the party introduced new rules to make leadership changes more difficult, the underlying culture of personality-driven politics remained. Albanese's leadership has so far avoided internal revolt, but it nonetheless remains subject to the same media and polling pressures that have shaped the political terrain for over a decade.

The cult of leadership also narrows the diversity of voices in public debate. When everything hinges on the leader, internal critics are marginalised, dissent is viewed as disloyalty, and alternative visions struggle to gain traction. Parliamentary democracy depends on contestation, deliberation and accountability, all of which are weakened when power is concentrated in the hands of one individual. The danger is not just instability but shallowness: a political system obsessed with the leader of the day, but indifferent to long-term reform or institutional renewal.

Rebalancing this dynamic will require a recalibration of political culture. Parties need to devolve power back to caucus members, empower ministers, and reassert the importance of collective decision-making. Journalists and analysts must move beyond leadership speculation to engage more deeply with policy substance and institutional context. And the public must demand more than a slick media performance or favourable poll numbers. The health of Australian democracy depends on moving past personality politics and rediscovering the strength of the parliamentary system itself.

The Architecture of Disillusionment

What emerges from this analysis is a political system not merely adrift but actively hollowing itself out. The weakening of ideology, the collapse of internal party democracy, the marginalisation of policy and the elevation of personality above principle. These aren't isolated developments, they're structural features of a political culture that has prioritised tactics over vision and survival over substance. The result is a Parliament filled with careerists rather than conviction politicians, parties that no longer represent coherent worldviews, and voters who no longer believe their engagement can effect real change.

This is not just a crisis of leadership. It's a crisis of purpose. Institutions designed to channel democratic will are instead servicing self-preserving elites. Once proud political parties — engines of debate, reform, and social transformation — now serve as branding vehicles for electioneering, with policy platforms treated as optional extras. And as the traditional frameworks of ideological identity have eroded, voters are left searching for meaning in a system that appears increasingly transactional and unmoored.

Yet even within this malaise, the system continues to function, at least procedurally. Elections are held, governments formed, legislation passed. But the deeper question is to what end? If politics has become an end in itself, rather than a means to public good, then it is not just policy outcomes that suffer, it is democracy itself.

The next chapter turns from institutions to ideas, or more precisely the absence of them. Where once Australian politics was grounded in broad philosophical traditions and values, today it is marked by a thin pragmatism and reactive policymaking. Chapter 3 will examine the collapse of political conviction in greater detail, mapping how ideological erosion has not only reshaped the major parties but also created a vacuum into which populism, opportunism and shallow rhetoric have rushed to fill the void. If this chapter has dissected the shell of modern politics, the next explores its hollow core.

Chapter 3

THE COLLAPSE OF CONVICTION

The Quiet Retreat from Belief

The ideological foundations of Australian politics have quietly eroded, leaving behind a landscape dominated by managerialism, market-tested rhetoric and short-term pragmatism. What was once a contest of ideas has become a competition of tactics, with conviction steadily giving way to convenience. Political actors still invoke values, but increasingly these references are hollowed out: strategic rather than sincere, symbolic rather than substantive. The language of principle remains, but the commitment to principle is in retreat.

This chapter examines the steady decline of political conviction in Australia: how it happened, why it matters and what it reveals about the character of contemporary governance. The erosion has not occurred in isolation. It is the natural corollary of the institutional degradation explored in the previous chapter. The death of big ideas is not a coincidence, it is a symptom.

At the heart of this analysis is a concern with purpose. If political institutions no longer embody coherent philosophical frameworks, what animates their decisions? When parties jettison ideological anchors, they become reactive, opportunistic and transactional. The result is not just incoherence but a form of leadership without direction where decisions are made to survive the day rather than shape the future. If Australia is governed without conviction, then democracy itself risks being governed without meaning.

From Ideological Pillars to Policy Drift

Australian politics was once underpinned by grand ideological traditions. The Labor Party emerged from the labour movement with a clear commitment to collectivism, social equity and the power of the state to ameliorate inequality. The Liberal Party, in contrast, positioned itself as the party of individual freedom, economic liberalism and restrained government. These were not just branding tools, they were philosophical anchors. They shaped not only policy choices but also the internal discipline, candidate selection and long-term goals of each party.

Today, those anchors have come loose. The parties remain (still called Labor and Liberal, still competing for power) but the ideas that once differentiated them have eroded. Labor governs with market instincts; the Liberals legislate like technocrats. Ideological clarity has given way to a kind of policy drift, where decisions are increasingly made in response to polling, focus groups or media cycles rather than guided by enduring principles.

This is not merely about pragmatism by the way. All governments must compromise, but compromise used to occur within a framework of values. What's changed is the disappearance of that framework. The Liberal Party's economic philosophy, for example, has become increasingly incoherent. Once committed to small government, the party now supports massive subsidies for preferred industries. It champions deregulation in theory but expands bureaucracy in practice. Its rhetorical commitment to the free market often coexists with heavy-handed interventions and culture-war signalling that have little to do with liberalism in any classical sense.

Labor has undergone a similar transformation. Once the vanguard of progressive reform, the party has embraced a managerial style of governance that prioritises political safety over social ambition, as we explored in previous chapters. Its abandonment of bold redistributive policy, evident in the retreat from once talked about (from the safety of the Opposition) reforms to negative gearing and capital gains tax, speaks to a deeper caution. Even in areas of traditional Labor strength, such as industrial relations (for example the Rudd/Gillard 'fair work' reforms post work choices) and public service provision, the party has often failed to advance a compelling philosophical vision. The symbolism of fairness remains, but the substance is increasingly compromised.

This policy drift is not solely the result of electoral pressures. It reflects internal party cultures that have de-emphasised ideology in favour of electoral mechanics. The rise of professional political operatives (staffers, media advisers and campaign consultants) has changed the character of policy development. Rather than emerging from party rooms or grassroots debate, policies are often reverse-engineered from marginal seat polling. The aim is not to build a better Australia, but to survive the next news cycle or scrape together a majority.

In this context policy becomes transactional: an announcement here, a backflip there, a package designed to neutralise criticism or appease an interest group. There is little coherence between initiatives, because coherence is no longer the goal. The real ambition is to avoid mistakes, to defuse conflict and to stay on message. Policy is not viewed as a tool for social transformation but as a political liability to be managed.

This has left the electorate with little in the way of genuine choice. When both major parties converge in the centre, voters are left to differentiate on personality or competence, rather than values or vision. That is one reason why leadership matters so disproportionately in the current environment, as explored in the previous chapter. In the absence of ideological differentiation, personality becomes the substitute.

It is also one reason why minor parties and independents have gained traction. The rise of the Greens, the resurgence of One Nation, and the success of the Teal independents each reflect, in different ways, a rejection of the ideological vacuum at the centre. Voters are looking for coherence, for a sense that politicians stand for something. Even when these alternative voices fall short in execution, they often outperform the major parties in articulating a worldview.

The broader risk is that Australian politics becomes incapable of long-term planning. Without an ideological compass, policymaking becomes reactive rather than strategic. Challenges like climate change, housing affordability, tax reform or democratic renewal require more than short-term fixes. They demand a sense of purpose and direction. Yet in the current climate, governments lurch from one priority to the next, guided by political necessity rather than principled leadership.

This loss of conviction also affects how governments engage with complexity. Ideology, for all its flaws, provides a lens through which to interpret the world. A set of assumptions about human nature, society and the role of the state. Without that lens, governments are left responding to problems on a case-by-case basis, without a framework to prioritise or interpret. This not only weakens policy coherence, it makes reform politically incoherent.

The drift from ideological politics to tactical governance represents more than a change in tone. When parties stop asking what they stand for, they stop asking what government is for. Politics becomes a career path rather than a calling, and power is pursued for its own sake rather than for the pursuit of principle. This loss of ideological clarity has been reinforced by the rise of poll-driven governance, further cementing a political culture that is more interested in reaction than vision.

The Commodification of Political Messaging

If polling, as discussed in the previous chapter, is the compass of modern politics, then messaging is the vessel. Designed not for durability or direction, but for marketing appeal. Australian political communication has undergone a transformation: where messaging was once the means of conveying policy, it has become the central product. Politics is now sold like a commodity, with slogans substituting for substance and brand management overtaking governance.

This is not merely about political spin, it is about the reconfiguration of priorities within government. Media advisers now wield extraordinary influence, often rivalling or even eclipsing policy staff in importance. Cabinet deliberations are increasingly shaped by how an announcement will land in the 24-hour news cycle. I know this from the way cabinet ministers have discussed what goes on in the room. Complex policies are broken down into digestible soundbites, stripped of nuance to fit the contours of a headline or a social media grab. The logic is simple but corrosive: if a message cannot be marketed, it is not pursued.

This commodification of politics is deeply entrenched. Governments now allocate significant budgets to communications units, invest in market research firms, and employ consultants who specialise in narrative framing. Every policy is launched with a campaign mindset: logos are designed, talking points circulated, hashtags tested. Think about it, the journalists reporting on what politicians do have two access points: the politicians themselves and their media team. Policy advisers are nowhere to be seen in the process of communicating with the electorate. The machinery of modern governance increasingly resembles a corporate PR operation. The goal is not to inform, but to persuade, and more often than not to avoid scrutiny altogether.

One of the clearest illustrations of this shift came during the

Morrison government's "Operation Sovereign Borders" messaging, where the language of national security was deployed with deliberate vagueness. The lack of detail was the point: the strength of the message lay in its simplicity and emotional resonance. Policy was not something to be explained but projected. It was a brand. The same principle applied to slogans like "Back in Black," "Jobs and Growth," and "Building Our Future." These mantras dominated political discourse, often regardless of the underlying facts.

The Rudd-Gillard era also exemplified this trend. Rudd's "education revolution" and "building the education revolution" were clever turns of phrase but suffered from implementation issues that revealed the gap between message and outcome. The National Broadband Network, one of Labor's most ambitious infrastructure projects, was communicated poorly despite its potential, leading to a public understanding shaped more by political contest than by evidence. In both cases, messaging failed to support complex policy because it prioritised impact over explanation.

Even progressive causes have not been immune. The push for climate action, for example, has often been framed in emotive terms: "saving the planet," "climate emergency," "net zero by 2050", without corresponding clarity about trade-offs or implementation plans. While urgency is essential, the lack of substantive engagement risks reinforcing scepticism and enabling opposition messaging to characterise the issue as elitist or economically destructive. Without detail, even mere slogans are vulnerable.

The reliance on branding also alters the internal culture of politics. Aspiring politicians increasingly view communication skills as more important than policy expertise. Media training is prioritised over ideological development. The archetype of the modern candidate is someone who can "stay on message," rather than someone who can argue a case. This shift has a downstream effect on governance: when politics becomes performative, decision-making becomes defensive. Ministers speak in rehearsed lines, avoid detailed interviews (those that still exist) and sidestep scrutiny with practiced ambiguity.

It also encourages performative outrage. Media cycles reward conflict, and political messaging increasingly responds to this incentive structure. Instead of governing through deliberation parties govern through reaction, crafting responses to opponents' lines rather than pursuing an independent agenda. Outrage cycles become the new terrain of policy debate, reducing complex issues to morality plays or culture-war skirmishes. Messaging becomes not just commodified, but weaponised.

Social media has accelerated this phenomenon. Platforms like X, Facebook and Instagram reward brevity, emotion and virality. Political messaging has adapted accordingly, flattened into hashtags, memes, and reactive video clips. While this has democratised political expression in some ways, it has also incentivised superficiality, which is to say nothing about the rise of influencers taking up the time of politicians. The shelf life of a political message is now measured in hours, not weeks.

This shift also affects accountability. When messages become the primary political product, outcomes are secondary. A government can repeat a slogan about economic strength even as real wages stagnate, it can claim success on housing affordability while home ownership rates decline. Sound familiar? The consistency of the message, rather than the truth of it, becomes the standard. Think also about the lack of truthfulness in most negative political attacks. Political narratives are insulated from reality through sheer repetition, Labor's Mediscare campaign being a classic example.

There is an irony here. The more sophisticated political messaging becomes, the more transparent its artifice appears to the public. Voters are aware of the theatre, often detecting the rehearsed lines, the choreographed announcements and the studied outrage. And while such messaging may work in the short term, it deepens cynicism over time. Citizens begin to doubt not only the integrity of politicians, but the very possibility of honest political communication. Trust is therefore eroded.

There have been moments of rupture. The rise of independent candidates, for example the Teals, capitalised on public frustration with spin and sought to offer clarity, honesty and focus on local issues. While their own communications are not devoid of branding, they have generally avoided the hyper-professionalised messaging of the major parties. Their enduring success indicates a growing appetite for authenticity over choreography.

Yet the structural incentives remain. As long as political survival depends on news management and brand control, messaging will continue to shape governance in profound ways. The commodification of politics is not merely a communications issue, it is a democratic one. When message overtakes meaning, the public sphere becomes a stage and politics becomes theatre.

The next section turns to a related consequence of this hollowing-out: the avoidance of moral leadership. In a culture where messaging dominates and polling dictates caution, politicians are increasingly unwilling to take moral stands on difficult issues. The result is not just timidity, it is a failure of political character.

Moral Timidity and the Cost of Avoidance

Modern Australian politics is not simply marked by the absence of ideology or the dominance of spin, it is increasingly characterised by a distinct reluctance to take moral stands at all. This moral timidity reflects a broader failure of leadership: a political culture where courage is penalised, conviction is absent, and the avoidance of controversy is mistaken for prudence.

Moral leadership is not always about policy in the narrow sense. It is about setting direction, framing priorities and being willing to articulate and act on ethical imperatives, even when they are unpopular. Historically, this form of leadership has marked the country's most significant moments, from the post-war embrace of multiculturalism, to universal healthcare to the Stolen Generations, to the apology. In each case, political figures took risks that transcended the immediate calculus of popularity.

Today, however, such moments are rare. Australia's political leaders increasingly shy away from difficult conversations, especially those involving entrenched injustices or long-term ethical challenges. Climate change, refugee policy, Indigenous recognition, aged care and gambling reform are policy areas demanding a degree of moral clarity that is too often absent from political discourse. Instead, issues in these policy spaces are framed in technocratic or transactional terms, if they are addressed at all.

Such timidity is not accidental, it is a product of the institutional incentives explored earlier: polling that punishes risk-taking, media cycles that amplify outrage, and political advisers who urge caution above all else. But the consequence is a kind of ethical erosion. Governments begin to act not on the basis of what they believe is right, but on what they calculate can be sold. Even when confronted with moral crises — such as natural disasters, abuse in institutional care and racial injustice — the default posture is managed empathy followed by minimal intervention.

Asylum seeker policies have become a bipartisan exercise in moral evasion. Successive governments have prioritised deterrence over decency, with offshore processing, indefinite detention and secrecy becoming defining features of the system. These approaches are justified through appeals to border integrity and deterrence, but they come at the expense of international reputation and human dignity. What is striking is not just the policy itself, but the unwillingness of most political actors to even question its ethical foundations. It is treated as settled, untouchable and therefore no longer even up for serious debate.

Climate change, too, presents a test of moral leadership that has largely resulted in failure. While there is now broad rhetorical agreement about the need for action, the pace and ambition of policy have been constrained by political self-interest. Governments fear backlash from regional voters or resource sectors and so adopt half-measures: net zero targets without roadmaps, renewable transitions without structural adjustment. The result is a policy landscape defined by incrementalism, where symbolic gestures are substituted for systemic change.

This trend has also emerged in domestic social policy. The treatment of welfare recipients, for example, reveals a persistent unwillingness to defend the dignity of the unemployed or underemployed. The Robodebt scandal was not merely a bureaucratic failure, it was an ethical failure. A government automated cruelty, reversed the burden of proof, and pursued vulnerable Australians for debts that did not exist. The response, when the illegality was confirmed, was muted and managerial. Accountability was delayed, apology carefully phrased. It is difficult to imagine a clearer instance where moral clarity was required, yet it was withheld.

Even in foreign policy the same pattern applies. Australia has often avoided taking strong moral stands on international human rights issues when doing so might jeopardise trade relationships or diplomatic convenience. Statements are made in abstract terms: abuses are condemned with caution, action is rarely taken. The moral authority that Australia might wield is frequently sacrificed at the altar of economic realism.

What is lost in all of this is not just public trust, but a sense of what politics is for. In a democracy, leadership is not merely about reflecting public opinion, it is about shaping it. That includes making ethical arguments, explaining why certain decisions are necessary and accepting the costs that come with principle. When leaders decline to do so, they diminish not only their own authority, but the quality of public discourse. Citizens become cynical, disengaged or apathetic, not because they are uninterested in politics but because they no longer believe it is capable of producing anything meaningful.

It is worth noting that moral clarity does not always lead to electoral disaster. There are moments in Australian political history where ethical leadership has been rewarded. Paul Keating's 1992 Redfern Speech, while controversial at the time, came to define his legacy and came to be recognised as a moment of extraordinary moral insight. Kevin Rudd's apology to the Stolen Generations in February 2008, though overdue, was widely supported. These moments reveal that the public is capable of responding positively to ethical leadership, if only it is given the opportunity.

But such moments do require risk taking, and contemporary politics is structured to avoid it. The hollow state, in this sense, is not merely a description of institutional decay, it is a diagnosis of ethical retreat. The absence of purpose is not only intellectual but moral. Political actors have learned to avoid fights, dodge judgement and outsource their conscience to the mechanics of media strategy.

In the next section, we explore how this erosion of moral courage has impacted the internal life of political parties themselves. Once shaped by debate and conviction, party rooms have become increasingly transactional, driven by factionalism, careerism and opportunism. The result is a political class that reflects the system's hollowing out rather than resists it.

The Party Room as a Marketplace of Ambition

If political conviction has withered in public leadership, it has decayed even more profoundly within the private deliberations of the party room. Once a site of ideological contest, policy innovation and internal discipline, the party room has become a marketplace. One in which ambition is the currency and advancement the goal. The internal culture of Australia's major political parties reflects the broader hollowing-out of purpose, with factional allegiances and media profiles supplanting principles as the engines of career progression.

The historical role of the party room was not merely administrative. It was where philosophical positions were tested, leadership held to account, and policy directions contested. Internal debate, even when bruising, could improve decision-making and sharpen a party's strategic focus. Today much of that debate has been displaced by performance management: how a minister presents in the media, how a backbencher navigates factional loyalty, or how quickly a rising star can secure a frontbench opportunity. Merit, once connected to intellectual rigour or policy contribution, is increasingly defined by optics and loyalty.

Factionalism, while not new, has hardened into something more corrosive. In both major parties factions operate not as ideological clusters but as vehicles for advancement. Deals are made not on the basis of shared worldviews but based on transactional convenience. Support is traded not earned. Preselections are brokered by power blocs, not communities. The consequence is a system in which the brightest minds may be sidelined while the most compliant thrive. Dissent is discouraged unless it aligns with the tactical interests of a dominant faction.

The Liberal Party's experience in recent years illustrates this point. Historically a broad church spanning economic liberals, social conservatives and centrists, the party has become increasingly unstable due to ideological incoherence and factional contests for influence. The ascendancy of Scott Morrison, engineered through backroom manoeuvres and factional compromise, exemplified the transactional culture at the heart of contemporary party leadership. Morrison's appeal to multiple wings of the party was less about shared conviction than about malleability: he was not chosen because he stood for something, but because he could stand with anyone, and therefore offend no one too strongly. Of course that was then. Morrison eventually managed to offend everyone.

Labor, too, has suffered from similar dynamics. While its factional structure is more formalised, it has become increasingly distanced from the party's base. Union influence, once grounded in mass membership and industrial solidarity, has morphed into bureaucratic control by a handful of insiders. Talent pipelines are shaped less by workplace experience or community service than by time spent as a staffer, adviser or political organiser. The revolving door between backroom roles and parliamentary seats has created a professional political class that is both well-trained in internal politicking and ill-equipped to represent.

This careerism has several consequences. First, it produces risk-averse politicians whose principal concern is avoiding missteps rather than pursuing reform. Their speeches are cautious, their voting records obedient, their media performances over-rehearsed. Second, it fosters cynicism among party members and the broader public. When ambition is perceived to outweigh principle, trust erodes. Not just in individual politicians, but in the institutions they inhabit. Third, it narrows the talent pool. Those with diverse backgrounds (community leaders, academics, businesspeople or activists) may find the internal culture of party politics too alien or corrosive to endure.

There is also the question of discipline. In earlier eras, discipline was enforced not merely to manage messages but to protect the coherence of a governing philosophy. Today discipline is primarily enforced to avoid negative media coverage. The goal is containment not consistency. Parties therefore often suppress internal debate even on issues where open discussion would be constructive. Policy development becomes risk-averse or outsourced altogether, to consultants, think tanks or public service agencies whose roles have themselves been diminished.

The result is a hollow party structure with few members, lots of ambition amongst elected MPs but with little evidence of strong convictions. Australian parties, particularly the majors, are no longer mass movements. Their grassroots have shrunk, their internal mechanisms are opaque and their recruitment pipelines are increasingly narrow. The feedback loop between voters and party elites is weak. This has made the major parties more susceptible to public disaffection and more vulnerable to disruption, whether from independents, minor parties or anti-political sentiment.

Ironically, as ambition becomes the dominant force in the party room, leadership itself becomes less stable. Leaders are no longer protected by deep ideological or institutional loyalty. Instead, they are assessed tactically: on how they're polling, how they perform in the media and how they manage competing interests. This short-sighted thinking undermines both authority and strategy. Leaders govern under the constant threat of destabilisation and internal leaks, with their primary focus often directed inwards rather than outwards. Prime ministers fall, not because of seismic ideological shifts, but because of minor shifts in factional arithmetic or internal polling.

This culture also creates space for performative rebellion. MPs who see limited opportunity within party structures sometimes adopt provocative or maverick personas to increase media visibility. This behaviour often has little to do with genuine ideological dissent and more to do with brand-building. The rise of figures who style themselves as political "outsiders" while remaining deeply enmeshed in insider structures is one symptom of a broader dysfunction: politics as performance, even within the party room.

Despite this the hunger for authenticity remains strong, both among voters and within small sections of the parties themselves. The success of independent candidates in traditionally safe seats, the growth of issue-based movements and the rise of young, values-driven MPs suggest there is still a market for purpose in politics. The challenge is that these forces remain largely peripheral to the dominant machinery of ambition. Without serious internal reform, the party room will remain a place where conviction is rare and advancement is everything.

This chapter has traced the collapse of political conviction across Australian politics. From polling dependency to commodified messaging, moral evasion and the internal erosion of party integrity. Together, these developments explain why Australian democracy feels increasingly directionless. The state is not incapable of governing, it has simply forgotten how to do so with meaning.

In the next chapter we turn from internal political culture to the broader institutional landscape, examining how the public service itself has been drawn into this hollowing-out. What happens when the machinery of government is no longer protected from the same short term thinking and strategic drift afflicting its political masters?

Chapter 4

THE TRIUMPH OF TACTICS

Australian politics has become consumed by the short term. Tactical calculations have eclipsed strategic purpose, leaving behind a system that prioritises performance over policy and headlines over outcomes. While politics has always involved an element of gamesmanship, the balance has fundamentally shifted. What was once a tool of leadership has become a replacement. Strategy is no longer the framework within which tactics are deployed.

This transformation has not happened overnight, nor is it unique to Australia. But its impact here is pronounced, aided by the instability of leadership in recent decades and the professionalisation of political operations. Anthony Albanese has made much of his break from recent leadership instability: surviving a full term in opposition, followed by a full term in government, going on to win a resounding victory at the 2025 election.

But he did so by shrinking into the job of prime minister, proving himself a consequential example of what a leader becomes in the wake of the reshaping of Australian politics following years of instability. He is the definition of a hollow politician. Leaders no longer seek to shape the long arc of public life. Instead, they seek to navigate it or more accurately, survive it one news cycle at a time. The result is a governing class more skilled in the arts of political combat than in the crafting of public policy.

The consequences are profound. Policy has become reactive, reform is deferred or diluted, public trust continues to erode and political discourse is increasingly shallow, shaped by the rhythms of media engagement rather than democratic deliberation. Tactical success is often mistaken for good governance, even as the long-term challenges facing the country remain unaddressed. The fourth estate contribute to this with horse race style coverage.

This chapter explores how tactics have triumphed in Australian politics, not as a symptom of weakness, but as a defining feature of the political system. It examines the abandonment of strategy, the rise of permanent campaigning, the dominance of polling and focus groups, the weaponisation of cultural division and the ultimate cost of governing without vision.

Strategy Abandoned

Politics in Australia was once defined by long-term ambition. Grand projects, structural reform and visionary leadership formed the bedrock of public life. From nation-building infrastructure to comprehensive economic overhauls, the political class sought not just to govern, but to shape the future. To keep Australia ahead of the pack by embracing the difficult decisions before it was too late. That era is gone. In its place stands a tactical class: reactive, opportunistic and perpetually focused on the next headline or poll bounce. Strategy has not simply been neglected, it has been actively abandoned.

The shift is neither accidental nor benign. It reflects a structural transformation in how politics is practised, driven by changing media dynamics, the rise of professional political operatives, and a hollowing out of ideological convictions. Leaders are no longer expected to articulate a coherent vision or lay out multi-term policy agendas. Instead, they are judged by their ability to manage a crisis, neutralise opponents and win the news cycle. All while keeping one eye on the next election. The result is a political culture that prizes manoeuvre over real meaning.

This tactical mindset is not limited to moments of electoral pressure, it has become a permanent feature of the political landscape. Governing parties operate in a state of permanent campaign, a concept Thomas Mann and Normal Ornstein first identified at the turn of the century happening in the United States. It happens when short-term advantage trumps long-term consequences. Policy development, once the domain of ministers and bureaucrats in deliberative processes, has been subordinated to the calculations of media advisers and strategists. Even cabinet decisions are increasingly shaped, not by principle, but by political optics. For example how will this play out in marginal seats? What will the newspaper tabloids say? How will it poll in Western Sydney or the outer suburbs of Melbourne?

The abandonment of strategy is evident in the churn of policy initiatives that vanish as quickly as they are announced. Announcements without follow-through, reviews that gather dust on shelves after being commissioned to much fanfare. Reforms get junked at the first sign of resistance even when ideas do occasionally manifest in action. Complex problems are usually met with simple slogans and symbolic gestures are mistaken for substantive action. It is not just that politics has become more cynical, governing has become indistinguishable from campaigning.

A clear example of this dynamic was Scott Morrison's embrace of "quiet Australians," a rhetorical device deployed not to define a long-term vision for the country but to frame a single electoral contest. It was a message designed for the moment, with little policy weight behind it. Who can recall the substantive policies that the Morrison government calibrated to appeal to this electoral cohort?

Similarly, the 2022 Labor campaign under Anthony Albanese was striking for its tactical restraint. Promising only incremental change, it was less a vision for Australia's future than a strategy to avoid risk. The entire campaign was an exercise in not losing — eking out a victory by not being Scott Morrison — a symptom of a political culture where playing it safe is preferable to offering substance.

By contrast, the Hawke-Keating governments offer a reminder of what strategic political leadership once looked like. Economic reform under their leadership was not universally popular at the time. Indeed, much of it was electorally dangerous, but it was underpinned by a clear sense of purpose and a willingness to expend political capital for long-term gain. The introduction of compulsory superannuation, the deregulation of financial markets, the floating of the dollar. None of these could have been delivered in the current political climate, where survival is paramount and tough choices are avoided like a plague.

The abandonment of strategy has consequences not only for governance but for democratic legitimacy itself. Citizens increasingly perceive politicians as insincere, driven more by spin than by substance. They aren't wrong by the way. Trust in institutions continues to decline, in part because the public (correctly) senses that decisions are being made for tactical reasons rather than principled ones. When politicians behave like marketers, the public treats them as such: with scepticism, and increasingly, with contempt.

This cynicism is further fuelled by the narrowing of voices within political parties we've already discussed and will return to in Chapter 8. With factional power brokers and political staffers dominating preselection processes, the number of parliamentarians with genuine policy expertise or reformist ambition has dwindled. Those who might once have entered politics to advance a particular cause or pursue meaningful reform now find themselves marginalised unless they play the tactical game. Ambition, where it exists, is personal rather than programmatic. A quest for leadership, not a true legacy to be proud of.

As a result, even leaders with genuine policy instincts find themselves hemmed in by the constraints of a tactical system. The internal logic of contemporary politics discourages boldness, punishes missteps ruthlessly and rewards the ability to navigate complexity without ever resolving it. Strategy, once the currency of political leadership, has become a historical footnote. In its place it's tactics, tactics, tactics.

The 24-Hour Campaign

The modern political cycle no longer allows for pauses, it never switches off. What was once a concentrated period of activity in the lead-up to elections has become a permanent condition. We now live in a world of permanent campaigning, where political leaders and their staff operate as though they are always just one news cycles away from potential disaster. The rhythms of governance have been displaced by the tempo of media management. The campaign never ends, it simply morphs from one tactical engagement to the next.

In this environment, substance is easily sacrificed. Policy becomes secondary to presentation. Leaders become more known for their image than their ideas. Political decisions are no longer guided by deliberation or considered judgement but by how they will play on the nightly news or trend on social media. As a result, ministers and their staff treat government announcements like campaign soundbites, not serious contributions to long-term governance.

The rise of the 24-hour campaign is inseparable from the evolution of the media landscape. Once, political communication followed a predictable rhythm: daily newspapers, morning radio followed by evening news bulletins. Now with rolling news coverage, talkback radio, live blogs, online outlets and the unrelenting noise of social media, there is simply no escape. Politicians are pressured to respond to every issue, every accusation, every rumour, all in real time. The space for reflection or strategic thinking is non-existent. Silence is treated as weakness and speed, not substance, becomes the defining virtue.

In a 2021 piece I wrote for *The Australian*, I observed that this constant campaigning has changed the very culture of political leadership. Ministers now spend more time prepping for media appearances than they do reading departmental briefs. Backbenchers are trained not in policy development, but in message discipline and media avoidance. This has given rise to a generation of politicians skilled at surviving but ill-equipped to govern. They are fluent in spin, cautious to a fault, and deeply risk-averse. That's not an accident, it's the natural outcome of a political system geared around tactics not ideas.

The Morrison government was particularly adept at this permanent campaign mode. Its obsession with marketing — from the creation of the "Prime Minister for Sydney" moniker to its hyper-controlled announcements — revealed a government more interested in managing impressions than pursuing policy substance. It was government by photo-op, driven by tactical imperatives rather than any clear program of reform. The "announceable" replaced the deliverable. And when something went wrong, it was spun away or reframed rather than confronted. That wasn't unique to Morrison, but he took it to its logical conclusion.

Labor under Albanese has followed a similar template, albeit with a more restrained tone. The 2022 election campaign, which essentially extended for the first two years of government, was characterised by caution. Promising as little as possible after the failure of the Voice referendum — after halfway through the term of government — in October 2023 and avoiding risk became the core strategy. Once in office, Labor prioritised keeping expectations low and message control high. For all the talk of resetting the tone in Canberra, the government remained tightly wedged between managing perceptions and preserving political capital. It is a politics of low ambition, shaped by the constraints of a 24-hour campaign culture and a low brow media environment.

This permanent campaigning mindset distorts more than just communication. It affects policymaking timelines, parliamentary behaviour, and public expectations. Legislation is rushed or deferred depending on media interest. Parliamentary Question Time becomes little more than a theatre of tactical point-scoring. Even budgets, once detailed blueprints for governing, are framed in terms of how they will "land" politically rather than what they seek to achieve economically or socially. The key question is no longer: "What is the right thing to do?" but "How will it play?"

The consequences are visible in the erosion of public trust. Voters may not follow every twist of the media cycle, but they can sense when politicians are faking it. When every appearance is choreographed, every answer rehearsed, and every action designed for political effect, authenticity evaporates. Politics begins to feel like a performance, and citizens unsurprisingly disengage. The rise of populist figures and anti-political sentiment is in part a response to this hyper-tactical environment. People crave purpose, not just political positioning.

In this climate, even well-meaning reformers struggle to cut through. Ideas that require time to explain or that involve complexity are easily crowded out by the demands of the immediate. Attention spans, within government and among the electorate and media, are short. The tyranny of the urgent wins out over the importance of the long term. And so, the cycle continues: announcements, spin, reaction, repeat.

Governance, in its truest sense, requires space to think, consult, plan, and lead. But in a politics dominated by the 24-hour campaign, that space no longer exists. Leaders are trapped in a loop of tactical calculation, unable to lift their gaze beyond the next media hit. It's a failure not just of individual leadership but of the system itself. A system that now rewards the superficial over substance and reacting over showing resolve.

Polls, Focus Groups and Fear

One of the clearest signs of the triumph of tactics in Australian politics is the centrality of polling and focus groups in shaping not just electoral strategy as discussed, but the day-to-day functioning of government. We've touched on this in earlier chapters. Once seen as tools to supplement political judgement, such research has become a substitute for it. Decisions are routinely tested against polling data, and political leaders increasingly defer to the findings of research consultants rather than the advice of public servants or the weight of expert evidence. Popularity is now the benchmark of legitimacy, and fear of a backlash drives policy retreat.

This dynamic has hollowed out political leadership. Politicians no longer lead public opinion, they follow it. And not just general opinion, but the curated, micro-targeted sentiments of swing voters in marginal seats. The delegate model of representation has been taken to a vacuous extreme. Focus group feedback has become the modern-day oracle, consulted obsessively to test language, refine messaging and pre-empt controversy. It is politics by proxy, and it creates a culture of fear: Fear of missteps, bad headlines, of the wrong word triggering the wrong reaction from the wrong voter.

In theory, there is nothing inherently wrong with politicians wanting to stay in touch with voter sentiment. In a representative democracy, understanding the public mood should inform good policy. But in practice, the reliance on polls and focus groups has become pathological. Rather than use them to guide communication strategies around principled decisions, governments now make decisions only if they first pass the focus group test. Courageous leadership — of the kind that persuades, educates and occasionally confronts — has become a casualty of this culture.

John Howard famously said he didn't need focus groups to tell him what he believed. He still used them, of course, but as a supplement, not a crutch. To know how to sell difficult policies to a wary electorate, or sometimes when to retreat from ideas to which the timing didn't lend itself. By contrast, more recent leaders have often treated polling as the first and last word in political judgement. This is not a reflection of strong democratic engagement, it is a symptom of institutional weakness. The fear of losing office now so dominates political thinking that any policy that risks a potential backlash is shelved or reframed until rendered virtually meaningless.

The 2010s were a high-water mark for poll-driven politics. Leaders were replaced not because they lost elections but because their approval ratings slipped. Kevin Rudd, Julia Gillard, Tony Abbott and Malcolm Turnbull were all casualties of internal polling as much as public perception. They also used it from time to time to vanquish internal opponents. I guess for some of these leaders what goes around comes around. The revolving door of leadership created a culture of hypersensitivity to public opinion. In such a climate, no decision could be made unless it was politically bulletproof. Reform lost out.

This pattern has extended well beyond leadership changes. Take tax reform, for example. Despite overwhelming consensus amongst tax experts on the need to broaden the base and improve equity, particularly around superannuation tax concessions and capital gains taxes, governments have repeatedly pulled back from action due to fears about negative polling. Labor's foray into super reforms — the taxing of unrealised gains — has ignored expert advice and is fundamentally flawed in its design. Even modest proposals, like Labor's franking credits policy in 2019, have been weaponised with such ferocity that parties are now more inclined to avoid detail altogether. Policy retreat is the path of least resistance.

The same applies to social reforms. Marriage equality, climate action and Indigenous recognition all required a level of political courage to advance, often against the instincts of focus groups in their early stages. But that kind of conviction-led politics is increasingly rare. When it has happened the shield of popularity has been used (a plebiscite for marriage equality), or failure has resulted in future policy retreat (think the aftermath of the Voice referendum). Instead, the dominant instinct is more often one of risk minimisation fuelled by market research. The result is not just a narrowing of debate, but a stunting of ambition.

This over-reliance on polling and focus groups has a self-reinforcing effect. Because decisions are framed by what is palatable, the public is rarely challenged. And because they are not challenged, their views remain untested. Politicians interpret this as proof that certain reforms are too risky, reinforcing their reluctance to lead. It is a cycle of mutual abdication: politicians decline to lead, and voters no longer expect them to.

Market research dependence has also shaped the behaviour of political staffers and party officials. Campaign directors operate like data analysts, segmenting the electorate into ever more specific slices, crafting messages that speak to each without contradiction. It is a form of political compartmentalisation: leaders say different things to different audiences and hope never to be held to account for the inconsistency. But voters aren't stupid. They detect the hedging, the evasions and the calculated ambiguity. And their trust in the system erodes further.

There's also a financial incentive driving this trend. The polling industry has become a staple of political operations, with lucrative contracts awarded to firms that can test messages, trial policy framing, and offer insight into voter psychology. Media outlets, too, use polling not just as a reporting tool, but as a means of shaping political narratives. This creates an echo chamber: politicians respond to the polls, the media report on the response, and the next poll reflects the reaction to the coverage. It's a feedback loop with little room for leadership. A the polling agencies spruik for corporate work by feeding the public use of political polling and research.

What's missing in all of this is conviction. Not blind ideology, but a coherent sense of purpose. A willingness to articulate a position and stand by it even if it comes at a political cost. The Hawke and Keating governments were not indifferent to polls, but they were willing to lead public opinion, not just chase it. The Howard government was too. Today, such leadership is all too rare. What remains is politics driven by fear: of unpopularity, of controversy and of electoral defeat.

Culture Wars as Cover

When conviction is absent and long-term policy reform is too risky, culture wars provide a convenient substitute. They offer politicians a way to appear principled without requiring policy depth. They generate headlines, galvanise partisan support and provoke opponents, all without necessitating meaningful legislative outcomes. In short, they are the perfect vehicle for tactical politics: high in visibility, low in responsibility. And they go both ways, with the left and the right happy to engage in them.

Culture wars are rarely about the issues themselves. Whether it's debates over gender identity, free speech, Australia Day or academic "wokeness," the point is not to resolve these matters but to exploit them. They become weapons of distraction, allowing governments to avoid confronting more difficult policy questions such as economic reform, structural inequality or the decline of public services. They do this by shifting attention to emotionally charged but politically safer ground. It's a classic sleight of hand: provoke outrage, then claim to be defending mainstream values against radical forces.

The Abbott government perfected this approach. While it failed to deliver coherent economic reform and stumbled on climate and education policy, it invested significant political energy into cultural signalling: attacking the ABC, targeting Safe Schools, and manufacturing controversy around national identity. These skirmishes served a political purpose. They energised conservative media outlets, baited progressive opponents, and allowed ministers to perform conviction politicking without needing to confront the complexities of actual policy delivery.

The Morrison government took a more performative approach. Morrison himself often projected a studied indifference to such debates, positioning himself as a suburban everyman uninterested in ideological warfare while quietly allowing ministers and backbenchers to prosecute cultural battles on his behalf. From Peter Dutton's interventions on race and law enforcement to Alan Tudge's attacks on universities, the government maintained a rolling culture war front that served as political cover during periods of policy drift or scandal.

These conflicts also serve an internal party management function. In an era when the Coalition is ideologically fragmented and Labor remains wary of its right flank, culture war posturing provides a lowest-common-denominator form of cohesion. It allows politicians with few shared policy commitments to unite around symbolic gestures: defending statues, criticising elites, or invoking "common sense" against supposed fringe activism. The substance is thin, but the politics is potent.

Labor, while traditionally more cautious in this space, is not immune to the lure of cultural tactics. In opposition, it often sought to avoid engaging in these debates altogether, fearful of being wedged. In government, however, it has tried to outflank the Coalition on values while steering clear of cultural controversies likely to alienate outer-suburban or regional voters. The result is often a confused and reactive stance, one that tries to satisfy both progressive and conservative constituencies and ends up pleasing neither.

The real danger of culture war politics is not just that it distracts from real policy issues, but that it distorts them. Education becomes a debate about curriculum bias. Climate action is framed as elitist moralising. Migration policy turns on identity and fear, not economics or humanitarianism. Complex issues are reduced to simplistic binaries, and the space for reasoned debate shrinks smaller and smaller. Political leaders no longer explain their positions, instead they caricature their opponents with negative attacks. Labor did this successfully during the 2025 election campaign. The result is a toxic political environment in which compromise becomes weakness and nuance is lost.

The media plays an amplifying role. Culture war flashpoints are ideal for clickbait journalism. They produce viral outrage, endless commentary and a sense of tribal belonging that drives engagement. Politicians know this, and many now stage-manage cultural skirmishes for media effect. A press conference mention of "cancel culture" or "radical gender theory" is guaranteed airtime, even if there's no legislative intent behind it. It's politics as performance art and it plays well to the algorithm.

This is not to suggest that cultural issues don't matter. Many of the debates that fall under the culture war umbrella touch on deeply important questions of identity, belonging and justice. But the way they are politicised often serves as an injustice to their complexity. Rather than engaging seriously with Indigenous recognition, for example, political actors reduce it to a binary for or against "the Voice." Instead of addressing the structural realities of inequality, the focus shifts to symbolic gestures and imagined threats to "mainstream values." Again, both sides of the culture war fall victim to this.

The Voice referendum became a casualty of this dynamic. What began as a modest constitutional proposal rooted in years of consultation and consensus-building was swiftly reframed as a polarising culture war battle. Opponents invoked fears of division and special treatment. Supporters struggled to mount a campaign that connected emotionally with a sceptical public. Political leaders across the spectrum tiptoed around the issue, wary of alienating voters. In the end, the referendum failed in every state with a 60 percent no vote nationally. Not necessarily because Australians rejected reconciliation, but because the political environment was too polluted by tactical calculations and cultural wedge politics on both sides.

Culture wars generate heat, rally the base and dominate the headlines. They present the illusion of importance but they don't solve problems. They don't build institutions, improve services or lift productivity. And they come at a cost because public debate is poisoned, communities are divided and politics drifts even further from real purpose. Tactical victories are won, but strategic ground is inevitably lost, and with each new skirmish the hollowing out of democratic life deepens.

In the absence of conviction culture wars are what fills the vacuum. But they are no substitute for real politics. They are a symptom of the system's failure to confront complex problems. Until that changes, cultural distraction will continue to thrive, not because voters demand it but because leaders lack the will to do otherwise.

The Cost of Governing Without Vision

There is a high cost to politics untethered from purpose. When tactical manoeuvring replaces strategic thinking, and when political survival becomes the only guiding principle, governments become reactive rather than proactive. They drift, avoid hard choices and ultimately fail to shape the future in meaningful ways. The result isn't just inertia it's decline. Decline in public trust, in institutional competence and in the capacity of the political class to meet the challenges of the day.

Policy atrophies in such an environment. Without a guiding philosophy or long-term plan, decisions are made to appease special interests, placate media cycles or neutralise opponents, not to solve problems. Governments become risk-averse to the point of paralysis. Proposals are floated, tested and shelved. Consultations are launched not to inform, but to justify deferral. Reforms are diluted beyond recognition or quietly abandoned altogether. The machinery of government still turns but it produces very little.

This is not a matter of ideological disagreement. There is absolutely space for robust contestation between left and right, progressive and conservative. But that contestation requires clarity of belief, objectives and intent. When both major parties are driven by tactical calculation above all else, the differences between them become performative rather than substantive. A case of Tweedle Dee verses Tweedle Dum.

That kind of politics erodes public engagement. Voters may still turn out at elections, because they have to, but increasingly they do so without enthusiasm or hope. And I say that as someone in favour of compulsory voting. Trust in institutions declines, and cynicism sets in. People come to believe, not entirely without reason, that politicians are more concerned with staying in power than using it. The idea of politics as public service is replaced by politics as a career. And in that environment, the best people often don't even bother to run.

The hollowing out of vision also undermines the public service. When governments lack a strategic agenda the bureaucracy is left adrift. Departments are told to implement shifting priorities based on polling not long-term objectives. Senior public servants are increasingly chosen for their political reliability rather than their policy expertise. The demarcation between public administration and political messaging blurs. Evidence-based advice is overridden by comms-tested positioning. The system becomes less capable, less independent and less resilient. Who would have thought that all these years later we are silently crying out for a return to a *Yes Minister* style public service forced to kowtow to the political class?

Crucially, the cost of governing without vision is most acutely felt in moments of crisis. A government that governs by focus group may muddle through in good times, but when a genuine emergency arrives, such as a pandemic, a global downturn. a bushfire or a flood, the need for leadership is immediate and non-negotiable. Tactics won't suffice, messaging won't mask failure. The test of vision is whether a government can act with purpose when it matters most.

The early phases of the COVID-19 pandemic revealed this tension. Australia's initial response benefited from competent public health infrastructure and a relatively compliant public, alongside our geographical isolation of course. But over time, tactical politics crept in. National Cabinet, which began as a promising forum for coordination, degenerated into a platform for blame-shifting and jurisdictional point-scoring. Vaccine procurement decisions were politicised. State and federal leaders traded barbs while pretending to cooperate before even that pretence fell away. Strategic clarity gave way to reactive messaging. A crisis that demanded unity and purpose was instead over time subsumed by the same short-term instincts that dominate normal politics.

Climate change presents an even starker example. The long-term nature of the problem has made it uniquely vulnerable to tactical delay. Governments have repeatedly framed climate policy as a choice between jobs and the environment, rather than an opportunity for transformation. The rhetoric changes, but the fundamentals don't. Interim targets are announced without credible pathways, industry is left uncertain, communities are pitted against one another and the window for effective action keeps narrowing. The same may have happened when it comes to an embrace of nuclear power, after years of delay to even put the issue on the agenda for proper consideration.

Governing without vision impoverishes our national conversation. Instead of debates about the kind of society we want to build, we get arguments about who leaked to whom, who won the week and which minister misspoke. Question Time becomes mere theatre, policy launches are media events and long-term reform agendas are replaced with retail politics designed for evening bulletins. This isn't simply a change in tone, it is a fundamental shift in what politics is used for.

At its best, politics should offer a contest of ideas, providing a space where competing visions for the future are debated before being tested at the ballot box. That requires courage: to set forth an agenda, stick to it, and persuade the public of its merit. It also requires patience, because real change takes time. The obsession with tactics has made that kind of politics increasingly rare.

And yet I believe there is still a public appetite for purpose. Australians don't demand ideological purity. They don't expect perfection. But they do expect leadership, not in the sense of "strongman" politics, but in the form of clarity, integrity and a willingness to say what you believe even if it costs you votes. The success of independents and minor parties in recent elections, particularly those who ran on platforms of integrity and climate action, suggests that voters are hungry for something more than spin. Of course whether those minor parties and independents are ultimately doing more than spinning with greater fraudulence remains up in the air.

The cost of governing without vision is not just political it is civic. It corrodes our shared understanding of what government is really for. It alienates citizens and lowers expectations, and it leaves the nation less prepared for the challenges that lie ahead. If politics continues down this path, the damage won't just be measured in policy failures but in the fraying of the democratic fabric itself. Tactics win elections but without vision they cannot sustain a nation.

Chapter 5
THE CULT OF PERSONALITY

Introduction

In a political landscape hollowed out by the triumph of tactics, the rise of personality politics is less a disruption than a logical progression. As conviction recedes and substantive policy debate thins, political identity increasingly becomes a matter of individual branding. Leaders are not judged by the depth of their ideas or the coherence of their agendas, but by their relatability, their media presence and their ability to embody a narrative (however shallow) that resonates with voters. We saw Peter Dutton fall victim to this cult of personality.

This transformation is not unique to Australia, but it has found fertile ground here. A 24-hour media cycle hungry for personalities, the decline of party membership and ideological coherence, and the media obsession of politics have all converged to make leadership more about projection than persuasion. The politician becomes a product, the campaign a marketing exercise and governing a performance designed to sustain image rather than deliver reform.

The consequences are profound. Political leaders increasingly prioritise personal popularity over institutional reform, shaping their agendas (or abandoning them altogether) based on what polls best. Cabinet becomes a stage for the prime minister rather than a forum for collective decision-making. Ministers fade into the background as the leader's persona takes precedence. Loyalty to a set of beliefs is replaced by loyalty to the individual. And the inevitable result is more fragility, more volatility, and more dysfunction.

This chapter examines how personality has eclipsed policy in modern Australian politics. It explores the evolution of the leader as celebrity, the role of the media in fuelling the cult of personality, the centralisation of power around political figureheads and the consequences for governance, accountability, and party cohesion. The question is not whether personal appeal matters in politics, it always has, but what happens when it becomes the only thing that matters.

From Party Leader to Brand

The shift from party leader to personal brand has redefined what it means to lead in Australian politics. Leaders are no longer simply the first among equals within a party room. They are marketed as the product itself: front and centre, omnipresent and increasingly detached from the institutions they ostensibly represent. This transformation hasn't just happened overnight, but its acceleration over the past two decades reflects a broader political hollowing out. The party is secondary, the brand is everything.

Modern political leadership is now filtered through the lens of celebrity. The traits that matter most — likability, media fluency, image discipline — are those most conducive to brand maintenance. Leaders are expected to be telegenic, emotionally accessible and performative with their authenticity. The result is a politics where content takes a backseat to presentation. Crafting an economic narrative or articulating a coherent reform agenda becomes less important than projecting the right aesthetic: relatable but authoritative, folksy but competent, scripted but seemingly spontaneous.

The media plays a critical role in this evolution. Journalists are drawn to personalities because they make better copy than often boring policy. The leader's gaffes, quirks or offhanded remarks garner more coverage than departmental briefings or white papers ever will. A leader who can command a press conference, deliver a zinger in Question Time, or go viral on social media is seen as more effective than one who quietly builds policy architecture or reshapes institutions.

This evolution also suits the internal power dynamics of modern parties. As the major parties have lost members, their internal democratic processes have weakened despite superficial claims to the contrary. The leader now dominates the party room, not through ideology or vision, but by controlling the flow of information, the public message and in many cases preselection processes. The result is a feedback loop: the more the leader becomes the party's brand, the more the party shapes itself around the leader's personality.

Kevin Rudd was a textbook example of this shift. He positioned himself as the outsider — the "man of the people" who had never been part of the Labor machine. His personal approval ratings soared, even as tensions with caucus and cabinet mounted. Rudd's downfall in 2010 wasn't due to policy failure or electoral unpopularity, although his timid retreat from climate action after having declared it the "greatest moral challenge" didn't help. But it was internal frustration at the centralisation of power and the dysfunction that came with a leader who ran government as a one-man show that really brought about Rudd's downfall. He was reinstalled three years later, not because of any substantive change, but because polling suggested his personal brand remained more saleable than the party's or Julia Gillard's.

The Coalition has not been immune either. Scott Morrison's tenure as prime minister was defined by his obsession with personal image. From the carefully cultivated "ScoMo" persona to his studied dagginess and choreographed empathy, Morrison was a leader who governed via marketing. His approach was intensely presidential, avoiding scrutiny with tightly controlling appearances, sidelining colleagues when their profiles risked overshadowing his own. Even Morrison's notorious line "I don't hold a hose, mate" was less a blunder than a reflection of the performative model of leadership he embodied. Governance was less about taking responsibility than maintaining brand coherence.

What is lost in this cult of personality is collective responsibility. Cabinet government becomes a formality rather than a decision-making engine. Ministers become background extras in the leader's narrative arc, trotted out to defend decisions they often didn't make or weren't even consulted on some of the time. The public service, meanwhile, is drawn into the orbit of the leader's office, expected to serve not the government of the day in a Westminster sense, but the personal political strategy of the leader. There have been plenty of scholarly books and articles written outlining the ways in which this transition has occurred. Governance becomes transactional and hyper-centralised.

There's also a subtle but important shift in how failure is understood. When leaders are brands, failure is treated like bad PR, something to be managed or spun away rather than confronted and corrected. The Morrison government's handling of the 2022 floods is a case in point: a moment requiring administrative competence and leadership instead became a matter of photo opportunities and media optics. A performative visit to a disaster zone took the place of meaningful engagement, as if leadership could be enacted through imagery alone. It felt like he was making up for his reaction to the 2020 bushfires which almost sunk Morrison's leadership.

The obsession with personality also weakens the ideological coherence of the parties themselves. Leaders are now chosen not for their alignment with party values or vision, but for their electoral appeal. Anthony Albanese, for instance, deliberately rebranded himself between opposition and government, from the combative inner-city leftist to the suburban moderate everyman. His party followed suit, trimming positions and muting ambitions in line with the new brand. What mattered was not the platform, but the packaging. Albo the party leader has been very different from Albo the former firebrand, even though he continues to immerse himself in internal factional wrangling.

The result is parties that change character depending on who leads them. Vision becomes malleable, priorities shift with polling. Party ideology, once the spine of political contest, is reduced to vague aspiration, subordinated to the needs of the leader's narrative. What remains is a politics defined not by purpose or principle, but by personality management and image control. A vacuous body politic.

Australia's political system was not designed for this kind of leadership. The Westminster model assumes collective responsibility, cabinet solidarity and accountability through party processes. Check and balances. But the reality is now presidential in style, without the structural checks that a presidential system might otherwise provide. There is no direct election of the executive, no separation of powers in the American sense, and limited means of challenging a prime minister whose grip on their party is rooted in media dominance and electoral branding.

This chapter continues by examining how media dynamics enable and reinforce this personality-driven model, and how the leader's image (often more than their policy) becomes the axis around which the entire political system now turns.

The Media Mirror

If politics has become a performance, then the media is both stage and spotlight. The transformation of political leadership into personality cults is inconceivable without the structural shifts in how media operates. From the 24-hour news cycle to the rise of social media, the platforms through which politics is mediated have reshaped the incentives for politicians. Visibility, not substance, is now the primary currency. And those who master the performance are often rewarded.

Commercial pressures on traditional media have played a central role in this dynamic, a topic we will return to in depth later on. As newsrooms shrink and journalists are expected to churn out content at pace, there is less time and fewer resources for in-depth policy reporting. Explainers, investigative pieces or detailed coverage of legislative reform give way to the faster, cheaper story: the gaffe, the clash, the meme moment. Leaders who can feed this demand for spectacle dominate the coverage. Those who cannot are sidelined, regardless of their competence or vision. I have done this myself, almost unwittingly, by rewarding those who play the game in a subconscious nod to how the system now works. It is hard not to be captured by it no matter where you are on the political stage.

Television, in particular, rewards personality. Leaders are judged by how they perform under pressure, how effectively they emote, how quickly they respond to a gotcha question. Scott Morrison's marketing background made him well attuned to this environment. His press conferences were tightly controlled, his appearances choreographed and his image carefully managed to maximise cut-through. Even during moments of crisis, such as the 2019–20 bushfires or the pandemic, messaging was crafted less around substance than on what would resonate in the nightly news bulletin.

Social media has taken this further. It offers a direct line to voters but also demands constant content. Leaders must project accessibility without appearing too rehearsed, show strength without arrogance, and authenticity even when it is being manufactured in a studio. The risk is that social media encourages shallowness, not just in the content itself but in the political thinking behind it. A 30-second clip or a shareable tweet becomes the measure of success. The algorithm becomes the arbiter of relevance.

It rewards those who can dominate the medium. Who can shape a narrative, spin an issue or pivot from failure with a pithy slogan or viral moment. It punishes those who dwell in nuance or who refuse to play the game. Malcolm Turnbull, despite his substantive policy interests, often struggled to control the narrative in a fragmented and fast-moving media environment. His attempts to bridge ideological divides or explain complex reforms were frequently drowned out by simpler, more aggressive messaging from within his own party or from the media outlets feeding off conflict. In the end he never developed the sort of substantial reform agenda huis supporters imagined he might.

The feedback loop inherent in the system is dangerous. Leaders tailor their personas to fit the media environment, while the media environment rewards those often vacuous personas. This creates a narrowing of acceptable political behaviour, where style triumphs over substance and where leaders fear appearing too complex, too honest or too uncertain. In an environment where perception is everything, policy ambition shrinks, reform becomes too risky and trying to explain complexity becomes a liability.

The result is a stifling sameness in leadership styles: the blokey everyman, the softly spoken moderate, the carefully curated underdog. These personas may differ in accent or posture, but all are bound by the same imperative: to remain on message, on brand and inoffensive to the middle ground.

This is not to suggest that politicians shouldn't communicate effectively. Nor is it to deny the importance of emotional intelligence or public engagement. Traits a number of failed leaders have lacked. But the current environment flips the priorities. The performance becomes the point. The message is shaped by what photographs well, not by what will govern effectively. The leader becomes a mirror, reflecting what the media (and the algorithms behind it) demand.

As the next section will explore, this shift has implications for how power is exercised and where it resides. The centralisation of authority around the leader's image — and the increasing marginalisation of ministers, backbenchers, and the public service — is not just a media phenomenon, it represents a structural transformation of governance.

Power Centralised, Cabinet Marginalised

As leadership becomes increasingly focused on personal branding, the machinery of government has been restructured, not formally but functionally, around the leader. In theory, Westminster democracy is built on collective responsibility where cabinet governs as a team and ministers are accountable for their portfolios. But in practice, the cult of personality centralises power in the prime minister's office, reducing cabinet to little more than a support act to the leader's performance.

This is a fundamental shift. Power has always been given to strong leaders, but traditionally that strength was measured through their ability to unify a cabinet, manage competing policy agendas and work within a party framework. Today, strength is more often defined by control: over messaging, over personnel, over access to the media. The Prime Minister's Office (PMO) functions less as a coordinating unit than a political war room, stage-managing the leader's image and insulating them from challenges, both external and internal.

This centralisation has practical consequences. Ministers are increasingly shut out of meaningful decision-making. Policy is announced without consultation. Major reforms are driven by the PMO or the leader's personal advisers, rather than through cabinet processes or departmental expertise. The public service, once a central pillar of Westminster government, is increasingly sidelined, valued more for its ability to deliver talking points than independent advice.

Julia Gillard's tenure illustrated both the strengths and weaknesses of resisting this model. Her government operated more traditionally, with stronger cabinet processes and a genuine commitment to ministerial autonomy. It was a response to Kevin Rudd's "gang of four" (made up of Rudd, Gillard, Treasurer Wayne Swan and Finance Minister Lindsay Tanner) which sidelined the previous cabinet. But she paid a political price for it. Her leadership style was less performative, more deliberative, and ultimately less compatible with the media's appetite for a singular narrative. Rudd, by contrast, concentrated power in his office to such a degree that ministers complained of being reduced to bystanders. The dysfunction that followed was not just interpersonal, it was structural. Born of a system where one man made all the decisions, sometimes without the courtesy of informing those tasked with defending them.

The Coalition governments under Abbott, Turnbull and Morrison continued this trend. Each, in their own way, centred the leader's persona at the heart of the political operation. Abbott's combative, campaign-style governance crowded out dissent and sidelined process. Turnbull, despite intentions to restore cabinet, often governed reactively, undermined by internal instability and media-driven narratives. Morrison, more than any recent prime minister, perfected the model of personalised, centralised power. His government was run from a bunker: tightly managed, heavily branded, and increasingly disconnected from the traditional checks and balances of cabinet and party room.

One of the most striking expressions of this centralisation emerged after Morrison left office. It was revealed he had secretly sworn himself into multiple ministerial portfolios, bypassing cabinet, colleagues and the public. The move, while extraordinary, was emblematic of a leadership style defined by control and secrecy. It showed the extent to which power had become concentrated in the leader, not just politically but administratively. The traditional structures of accountability — ministerial responsibility, parliamentary oversight and public transparency — had been sidelined in service of one man's political instincts.

This model of leadership also discourages independent talent. Rising MPs learn quickly that loyalty to the leader, not independent thinking, is the key to promotion. Ministers know their job security depends more on their media discipline than on portfolio performance. In fact they come to be seen as one and the same. Backbenchers are reduced to a chorus of brand amplification, expected to stay on message and avoid controversy. The party room becomes passive, with dissent seen as disloyalty and debate seen as destabilising.

Even within parties, power becomes increasingly presidential. Leadership spills are framed as coups against a singular figure rather than ideological contests or collective disagreements. The personalisation of power means that when leaders fall, entire governments often unravel, not because policy directions have changed but because the personal brand that held the edifice together has collapsed.

This is not just a Canberra problem, state politics reflects similar trends. Premier-led branding exercises dominate political messaging across state jurisdictions. Media advisers outnumber policy staffers in some ministerial offices. Leaders are increasingly treated as CEOs of the political enterprise rather than as first among equals in a collegial cabinet.

Importantly, this centralisation also weakens democratic accountability. When decisions are made behind closed doors, often by unelected staffers or a handful of insiders, the ability of parliament, the public service or the media to scrutinise them is diminished. Responsibility is blurred and ministers (rightly) deny involvement. Public servants are muzzled and the leader can either disavow decisions or spin them as personal triumphs, depending on the outcome.

The ultimate irony is that this style of leadership, while designed to project strength, often creates fragility. A leader who builds power solely around themselves lacks institutional resilience. When the brand falters, whether through scandal, electoral backlash or changing public sentiment, there's little left to fall back on.

Accountability Without Substance

When political leadership is reduced to performance and parties are hollowed out, the mechanisms of accountability begin to lose their teeth. The structures remain (press conferences, parliamentary question time, estimates hearings and watchdog bodies) but their capacity to hold power to account is diminished. What remains is often just theatre: the appearance of scrutiny without its substance.

In this environment, political accountability is managed rather than earned. Leaders face questions, but not necessarily consequences. Public statements are carefully constructed not to inform but to deflect. When things go wrong (and they routinely do) the instinct is not to explain or take responsibility, but to control the narrative.

This dynamic is amplified by the erosion of traditional mediators of accountability. The public service has been increasingly politicised, its independence eroded by a culture of loyalty to the government of the day. Ministerial advisers, unaccountable to parliament or the public, play gatekeeping roles that limit scrutiny and suppress dissenting advice. Watchdog bodies are often underfunded or ignored. Integrity is spoken of as a value but rarely treated as a constraint.

Consider the Morrison government's refusal to establish a robust national integrity commission. Promised, delayed, then diluted into irrelevance, the proposal became a symbol of performative accountability. The public wanted greater oversight. The government offered a model with limited powers, no public hearings and no retrospective jurisdiction. A body designed to appear tough while doing very little. It was accountability as image management, and Labor went along with it.

The media, too, struggles in this environment. Faced with declining resources and a 24-hour news cycle, journalists are often forced to trade depth for immediacy. Politicians exploit this by avoiding detailed interviews, flooding the zone with spin or selectively engaging with sympathetic outlets. When mistakes or scandals emerge, the goal is not to explain or apologise but to ride out the storm. In the absence of genuine party structures or policy platforms, there is little internal or external pressure to take responsibility.

Question Time, once a forum for genuine scrutiny, has become emblematic of the performative churn. It is now a daily ritual of rehearsed lines, planted questions and theatrical indignation. Ministers dodge, deflect or deny. Backbenchers play their part with soft questions and loud interjections.

Even when scrutiny does land via a damaging story, a leak or a public backlash, the response is too often procedural rather than principled. An inquiry may be announced, but its scope is narrow. A minister may resign, only to return months later in a different portfolio. Apologies are always conditional, admissions are very legalistic if they happen at all. The leader, shielded by layers of spin and staffers, invariably emerges unscathed.

This culture corrodes trust. Voters become cynical, not just about politics but about the possibility of meaningful accountability. The belief that leaders will act in the public interest and face consequences if they do not, is fundamental to democratic legitimacy. When that belief erodes, disengagement grows. Voters switch off, or worse they turn to populists who promise to disrupt the system entirely.

Yet even populists often adopt the same performative strategies. They rail against elites while carefully curating their image. They speak of authenticity while dodging hard questions. We see this on the left and the right. They may speak more directly but their leadership still hinges on personality over process.

None of this is inevitable. The structures of accountability can still work, but only if they are reinforced by a political culture that values truth, transparency and responsibility. That culture cannot be rebuilt through optics alone. It requires leaders willing to cede control, parties willing to empower their members, a media willing and able to dig deeper, and a public demanding more.

As we move into the next chapter — The Great Hollowing Out — the focus shifts from leadership and party to institutions more broadly. What happens when not just the political class, but the institutions of government themselves begin to lose purpose, capacity and legitimacy? If the cult of personality is a symptom, institutional decay is the disease it feeds on.

Chapter 6

THE GREAT HOLLOWING OUT

The decline of political conviction, the centralisation of power, and the personalisation of leadership are not isolated developments. They are symptoms of a deeper malaise: the hollowing out of institutional life in Australian democracy. From parliament to the public service, from statutory agencies to political parties, the structures designed to provide accountability, expertise, and continuity have been steadily weakened. Not by design, but by neglect, politicisation, and short term thinking.

This chapter shifts the lens from the individuals who dominate modern politics to the institutions they inhabit. Where once government was a system of interlocking checks and balances, today it operates more like a series of silos. Decision-making is centralised, scrutiny diluted, and institutional memory lost. As politics has become more performative, institutions have become less resilient, less respected, and in some cases, less relevant.

The causes are multifaceted. The rise of career politicians has coincided with a decline in the quality and independence of the public service. Parliamentary processes, increasingly stage-managed, have lost their deliberative edge. Meanwhile, the relentless churn of media cycles rewards spectacle over substance, compounding institutional fragility. What remains is a thin shell of democracy: the forms and rituals persist, but the foundations are eroding.

This chapter maps the contours of that erosion. It considers how the broader administrative state — in its contracts, consultancies, and outsourcing — reflects a withdrawal from long-term public stewardship. Finally, it explores the consequences of institutional decay for democracy itself: a growing vacuum of trust, purpose, and performance in public life. What emerges is a portrait of a system that retains the architecture of governance, but not the vitality.

The Theatre of Parliament

Parliament was once the epicentre of Australian political life, a forum where ideas were contested, national direction debated, and governments held to account. Today, its role has diminished to the point of near-irrelevance in shaping policy outcomes. Parliamentary debate is increasingly an exercise in theatrics, not deliberation. Question Time, in particular, has been reduced to a choreographed performance, more concerned with camera angles and media soundbites than ministerial accountability. Committees aren't much better.

The shift didn't happen overnight. It's been a gradual corrosion, accelerated by the growing dominance of executive government and the rise of political media management. Ministers arrive in the chamber with pre-approved lines. Backbenchers read from scripts. The cut and thrust of debate is replaced with slogans, insults, and rehearsed indignation. The theatre remains (the rituals, the rules, the grandiose architecture) but the substance has all but drained away.

This isn't just a matter of tone. The practical function of Parliament has been steadily hollowed out. Committee work is underfunded and underutilised even on the rare occasions it adds value. Bipartisan cooperation, once a quiet but vital feature of policy development, is now the exception. Question Time is no longer an instrument of scrutiny but a mechanism for messaging. Ministers dodge, deflect, or outright ignore questions, secure in the knowledge that the spectacle will dominate nightly news coverage, not the detail of their answers.

In this climate, oppositions have little incentive to engage constructively. The rewards for disruption and point-scoring outweigh those for policy engagement. The result is a vicious cycle: governments don't listen because oppositions don't offer serious alternatives, and oppositions don't try because governments don't engage in good faith. Parliament becomes little more than a backdrop for a 24-hour news loop that rewards outrage over insight.

Technology has worsened the effect. With instant news, social media amplification, and 24/7 commentary, the incentive structure for politicians is warped. Why engage in a nuanced debate when a viral zinger in the chamber will reach more people and win more headlines? Why craft a thoughtful speech when the only bit that matters is the thirty-second clip on Sky News or the ABC's evening wrap?

This change has bled into the internal workings of parties as well. The role of the backbencher, once vital in shaping policy through internal debate and committee work, has been neutered. Party discipline is enforced with ruthless efficiency, aided by media teams that monitor every utterance for signs of deviation. Members are less representatives than they are message carriers, deployed as needed to defend the leader's line or criticise the opposition on cue. Straying from the daily talking points is a sin.

Australians watching Parliament are less likely to see it as a functional institution of governance than as a combative, performative arena where little of consequence is achieved. And yet, Parliament's symbolic weight endures. It remains the physical and constitutional seat of Australian democracy. Its rituals and proceedings still matter, if only because they serve as the last formal checkpoint before laws are enacted. But formality is no substitute for function. If Parliament is increasingly sidelined in favour of executive decrees, late-night media drops, or policy-by-press-release, then its constitutional centrality becomes little more than an illusion.

The erosion of parliamentary power is not unique to Australia. Similar trends are observable in other Westminster democracies, from Canada to the UK. We will examine this in detail in our second to last chapter. But Australia's particular flavour of the hollow state has given rise to a more complete marginalisation. One where even significant legislative initiatives are often decided well before they reach the floor of the House.

This matters because it signals a deeper institutional decay. Parliament, at its best, is where public policy meets public accountability. It is where bad ideas are supposed to be exposed and good ones refined. When it fails in that role, not because of the building or the rules, but because of the people and the incentives driving them, the entire system is weakened. The electorate disengages, cynicism grows and trust in democracy declines.

The irony is that many parliamentarians themselves bemoan this state of affairs, often off the record away from the cameras. They speak of frustration, futility, and the sense that real decisions are made elsewhere: in cabinet, in party rooms, or more often, in leader's offices dominated by political staffers as we've discussed. But few are willing to challenge the system publicly, constrained by party loyalty, career ambitions, or simple fear of internal reprisals. And so the performance continues. Parliament remains, but its purpose is diluted. It becomes, like so much else in modern politics, an artefact of what once was. A hollow structure filled with noise but signifying little.

The Loss of Institutional Memory

One of the most corrosive but least visible consequences of the hollowing out of government is the gradual erosion of institutional memory. This isn't just a bureaucratic concern, it strikes at the heart of the state's capacity to govern effectively. To learn from its past and to avoid repeating them. When experience is devalued, when continuity is cast aside, and when political churn becomes the norm, governments become less capable and more reactive. They lurch from crisis to crisis without the benefit of hindsight or long-range thinking and planning.

Institutional memory is what allows governments to understand the context in which decisions are made. It ensures that lessons from past policy successes and failures inform current choices. It provides the historical depth and procedural knowledge needed for good governance. The ability to weigh trade-offs, to recall why certain reforms were tried or abandoned, and to build on what works rather than constantly reinventing the wheel. But in Australia, that memory is fading.

There are several reasons for this. One is the accelerating turnover in ministerial ranks. In recent decades, ministerial tenures have shortened significantly. Cabinets are reshuffled frequently, ministers cycle through portfolios at pace, and with each change, the learning curve begins anew. Institutional knowledge held at the political level (through lived experience, continuity of staff, and policy immersion) has become rare. Ministers now often rely on superficial briefing notes rather than deep engagement with the history of their departments or the issues they're tasked with overseeing.

Another reason is the rise of the political class at the expense of traditional expertise. Career trajectories that once brought professionals into politics after long experience in other fields have been replaced by political apprenticeships: Young staffers working their way up through ministerial offices, party machines, and think tanks. These operatives are skilled in the dark arts of political messaging and media management, but often lack grounding in policy development, administration, or institutional dynamics. The result is a political culture that prioritises short-term wins over long-term planning, with little regard for the historical context in which policies are being shaped.

This problem is compounded by the diminished role of the public service, a trend explored more fully later in the book. Public servants traditionally served as the custodians of institutional memory, providing governments with continuity, contextual knowledge, and an understanding of past efforts. But as their influence has waned and as departments have become more politicised and transient, so too has their capacity to perform this function. Long-serving officials with deep expertise are increasingly sidelined or replaced. Institutional knowledge is not being passed on, it's being lost.

Even within the departments themselves, constant restructuring has taken its toll. Organisational memory depends on stability. But public sector agencies have been repeatedly reshuffled, merged, and rebranded in the name of efficiency or political expediency. Functions are moved around, teams are broken up, units are closed. Staff are not retained long enough to develop the institutional knowledge that would once have defined a department's identity and purpose. With every machinery-of-government change comes a subtle amnesia, a forgetting of what came before.

The same dynamic is playing out in the world of political journalism and commentary. Fewer experienced political reporters are covering Canberra, and the turnover in press gallery ranks mirrors what's happening inside parliament itself. The ecosystem that once held institutional actors to account — journalists who had seen governments rise and fall, who remembered key policy battles, and who understood the dynamics behind decisions — is now less equipped to offer that depth. Instead, daily political coverage often mirrors the vacuousness of the politicians themselves.

This erosion of memory affects not just the internal workings of government, but also its ability to communicate effectively with the public. Citizens expect consistency and clarity from their leaders. But when governments forget their own history, they contradict themselves, repeat past failures, and appear directionless. That undermines trust. The public notices when governments launch initiatives that resemble earlier abandoned projects, or when ministers make statements that contradict long-held policy positions. Institutional forgetfulness becomes public farce.

The pandemic revealed just how costly this can be. In moments of crisis, governments need to draw on hard-earned lessons. Yet too often, pandemic responses were characterised by ad hoc decision-making, limited coordination, and a rediscovery of procedures that should have been embedded in institutional practice. National frameworks that had been developed for health emergencies were sometimes ignored or reinvented from scratch. The lack of institutional memory delayed effective action and diminished confidence in government responses.

Australia is not alone in facing this problem, but it is especially vulnerable because of the nature of its political culture. The centralisation of power in ministers and their offices, the decline of cabinet government, and the growing reliance on external consultants all contribute to a weakening of institutional knowledge. There are fewer places within the system where memory resides. And where it does exist it is often undervalued.

Reversing this trend won't be easy. It requires a cultural shift that recognises the value of experience, stability, and continuity. Not just in the public service but across the political class. It means rewarding depth over churn, embedding policy learning into institutional practices, and giving public servants the space and respect needed to advise frankly and carry lessons forward. It also means acknowledging that political leadership is not just about new ideas or bold reform, it's about remembering what has been tried, what has worked, and why.

The loss of institutional memory is rarely front-page news. It's not a scandal or a crisis. But it's a slow, steady weakening of the system's foundations. Without it, governments become less coherent, less capable, and more prone to repeating mistakes. In the end, no reform agenda, however well-intentioned, can succeed without the capacity to learn from the past. That capacity is what Australia's political institutions are increasingly missing.

The Outsourcing Addiction

Perhaps the most telling symptom of the hollow state is the extent to which government functions have been outsourced, not just operational tasks, but core elements of policy development and strategic planning. What began as a means to improve efficiency and bring in specialist expertise has, over time, become a crutch. Departments that once housed in-house capacity and policy brainpower now routinely turn to consulting firms for answers that were previously developed internally. The result is a public service less capable, less confident, and more dependent on external actors who operate beyond the traditional frameworks of public accountability.

This addiction to outsourcing is not accidental. It reflects a deeper mistrust of the public sector by some political leaders. A belief that the private sector is inherently more agile, innovative, or results-driven. But this ideological assumption has had damaging consequences. Rather than upskilling the bureaucracy or investing in institutional knowledge, governments have hollowed it out, and then paid private providers inflated fees to fill the void. The billions spent on consultants often deliver generic solutions, recycled frameworks, or reports that tell ministers what they want to hear.

Accountability suffers in this environment. Consultants are not bound by the same transparency requirements as public servants. Their advice is often commercial-in-confidence. Their contracts are shielded from scrutiny. If a policy fails responsibility is diffused. Blame can be pushed onto the consultants, who in turn retreat behind the protections of their engagement terms. Meanwhile, public servants lose the opportunity to learn from the experience, to adapt, or to build institutional wisdom that might inform future decisions.

The scale of this outsourcing has grown dramatically in recent decades. Once considered an occasional supplement to internal expertise, big consultancy firms have become entrenched players in government decision-making. In some agencies, consultants are effectively embedded, occupying roles indistinguishable from public servants. They help design programs, write policy briefs, and in some cases, even implement the very initiatives they have scoped, all while billing by the hour. The conflict of interest is not incidental, it's systemic.

This dynamic undermines not only public sector competence, but also democratic legitimacy. Voters are entitled to expect that decisions affecting their lives are made by those accountable to them, not by corporate consultants whose commercial interests may not align with the public good. The opacity surrounding consulting engagements — their cost, their terms, and their influence — corrodes trust. It fuels perceptions that government is captured, that expertise is for sale, and that private interests are shaping public policy from the shadows.

Attempts to rein in the influence of consultants have been largely performative. Budget papers might claim a reduction in "external labour hire," or ministers might promise to bring more work back in-house, but in practice the use of consultants remains embedded in the operating model of modern governance. Departments often lack the internal capability to deliver what is asked of them, creating a self-fulfilling dependency. Even when public servants know the answer, risk-averse leadership or politically sensitive ministers prefer the perceived neutrality (or plausible deniability) of external advice.

The consequences are far-reaching. Outsourcing drains resources that could be invested in building a high-performing public service. It creates a two-tiered system where core functions are split between under-resourced officials and well-compensated consultants. It distorts incentives, with career progression sometimes favouring those who manage outsourcing contracts rather than those who develop policy themselves. And it weakens the feedback loops that allow government to learn from its mistakes, because much of the knowledge generated is not retained within the system.

There is also a broader cultural impact. Over-reliance on external consultants signals to younger public servants that their ideas are less valued than those of private contractors. It reinforces a message that innovation is something to be purchased, not cultivated. This devalues the vocation of public service itself. Rather than encouraging bold thinking and long-term policy stewardship, it promotes short-termism and deference to external authorities, many of whom recycle imported models or offer politically convenient answers dressed up as independent analysis.

This culture of outsourcing extends beyond policy advice. Service delivery itself has been steadily privatised or contracted out, from employment services and aged care to disability support and vocational training. The results have often been mixed at best, with profit motives compromising quality, and accountability mechanisms proving rather weak. Yet even failures do not appear to stem the tide. Once a function is outsourced, it rarely returns to government. And when problems emerge, governments are more likely to commission a review from another consultant than to rebuild internal capability.

The hollowing out of government capacity through outsourcing mirrors a broader pattern of managerial drift. Ministers, increasingly drawn from a professional political class, often lack deep policy experience themselves. Senior bureaucrats, in turn, are incentivised to deliver politically palatable solutions rather than evidence-based advice. Into this void steps the consultants, offering slide decks, buzzwords, and an air of authority. But what's lost is the hard-won knowledge of how policy actually works in practice, how it can be adapted to local conditions, and how it should be developed and adopted over time.

The Morrison government's record illustrated this tendency in stark terms. From the (mis)handling of the vaccine rollout to the design of economic stimulus, consultants were front and centre. Firms were paid handsomely to do work that, in earlier eras, would have been the remit of line departments. Even emergency responses, such as those during the COVID-19 pandemic, were filtered through external advice, often at the expense of coordination and consistency. But the trend did not begin with Morrison, and it has not ended with him either.

Labor governments, too, have struggled to kick the habit. Rhetorical commitments to rebuilding public sector capability are rarely matched by decisive action. The political risks of failure, especially in complex policy areas, have lead ministers to fall back on external validation. And bureaucracies themselves, having lost much of their internal capacity, lack the confidence to assert their own expertise.

Breaking this addiction will require more than symbolic gestures. It will take sustained investment in people, training and institutional structures. It will also require a cultural shift that values long-term capability over short-term convenience, and that sees the public service not as a cost centre but as a vital national asset. Until then, the state will remain dependent on outsiders to do the work it has been hollowed out from within to perform itself.

From Westminster to Marketing Strategy

Australian democracy was built on the Westminster model, which presumes a functioning parliament, ministerial responsibility, and an independent, merit-based public service. But over time, that model has been diluted, if not disfigured. Increasingly, politics is less about process or principle and more about presentation. Announcements take precedence over outcomes, policy is filtered through the lens of polling as we've discussed, alongside media management and electoral strategy.

The transition from Westminster principles to marketing logic has affected all levels of government. The checks and balances that once characterised the system are increasingly circumvented. This has been accompanied by a rise in the political class: career politicians and advisers whose skillsets are honed in campaigning rather than policymaking. Their focus is on managing perception, minimising risk and framing opponents.

The result is not merely hollow rhetoric, but hollow governance. Initiatives are launched with fanfare, then quietly abandoned. Consultations are held, then ignored, such as the taxing of unrealised gains on superannuation. Trials are announced without implementation plans. Review recommendations are cherry-picked, as we saw with the Henry Review into the tax system during the Rudd era. What matters most is the appearance of action. Behind the curtain, there is often very little of substance being done.

Marketing logic also reshapes how public money is spent. Programs are designed not necessarily for maximum impact, but for maximum visibility. Infrastructure projects are timed around election cycles. Grants and funding announcements are targeted to marginal seats. Departmental resources are diverted towards communications and media teams. Public funds are used to bankroll government advertising that borders on party propaganda. It should all be illegal but the rules aren't written that way on purpose.

The whole process diminishes the integrity of the political system. Voters are treated as passive consumers rather than active citizens. Policy is delivered as a product, not as a social compact. The relationship between the government and the governed becomes transactional, with trust eroded each time substance fails to follow spin. Cynicism grows, and with it, disengagement. Voters are in turn won over by cynical spending to buy their support.

While all governments engage in political marketing, the scale and dominance of this approach in recent years represents a structural shift. What was once a supplementary function is now central. Leaders are judged not on their legislative achievements or administrative competence, but on their performance in front of a camera. Political survival becomes the organising principle of government.

This transformation helps explain the broader hollowing out of the state. Institutions are weakened not through direct attack, but through neglect. Parliament is sidelined, the public service is bypassed. What remains is a facade of democracy, appearances without the machinery to deliver substance.

The Normalisation of Incompetence

Perhaps the most corrosive outcome of the hollow state is the normalisation of mediocrity, or worse outright incompetence. In an environment where loyalty is prized over expertise, where short-term political wins outweigh long-term national interest, and where accountability mechanisms are eroded, it becomes possible for governments to consistently underperform without any consequences.

This isn't about individual ministers making occasional mistakes. It's about a system that no longer expects (or rewards) core competence.

Major policy failures become routine. Administrative bungles are managed, not resolved. Review after review highlight systemic weaknesses, yet little changes.

In some cases this is due to inexperience. A political class that moves swiftly from staffer to MP to minister may lack the depth or breadth of understanding that's necessary for complex portfolios. But the problem is deeper than this. Even capable ministers are constrained by the machinery around them: politicised advisers, weakened departments and a culture that discourages candour.

Mistakes, when they do occur, are rarely acknowledged. Spin overrides substance and blame is deflected or shifted down the chain. Responsibility is therefore obfuscated. Public confidence erodes as governments appear incapable not only of delivering on promises, but of admitting when they fall short. The Morrison government's handling of the vaccine rollout, the robo-debt scandal and the sports rorts affair are all case studies in failed governance in the traditional sense.

Yet the public becomes inured to this dysfunction. The expectation of effective government diminishes. Voters grow cynical, disengaged or fatalistic about what they see. Politicians are viewed not as leaders but as opportunists. Institutions are no longer trusted to deliver. A politicised public service lacks the independence or courage to push back. Outsourcing strips departments of institutional knowledge. The dominance of marketing strategies favours announcements over the quality of execution. And ministers, focused on political survival, often lack the incentives to invest in real reform or operational excellence.

Media fragmentation also plays a role. In a more cohesive media environment, failures would be relentlessly scrutinised across the political spectrum. Today, partisanship shapes most coverage. Scandals may be amplified or buried depending on ideological alignments. This distorts public understanding and reduces pressure for reform.

The cumulative effect is a political system that tolerates underperformance. In fact it has grown used to it. Ministers survive despite repeated failures, departments remain unreformed. Review recommendations gather dust and the cycle continues. Not because the problems are unsolvable, but because the system has ceased to expect higher standards of delivery.

Reversing this trend will take more than procedural tweaks. It requires a reassertion of public expectations: by the media, by civil society, and by voters. It also requires leadership, not just from those in office but from those within the system who still value competence, integrity and public service. Without that, the hollowing out becomes irreversible.

Chapter 7

'LEADERSHIP' WITHOUT LEGACY

Leadership in politics once meant something more than holding office. It implied vision, courage, and the willingness to expend political capital for the sake of long-term reform. Today, it often amounts to little more than survival. Australia has not been immune to this shift. Recent prime ministers have governed more like brand managers than nation-builders, focused on short-term optics, factional calculations and managing the 24-hour news cycle.

This chapter examines the modern political leader in Australia. It considers how the party room dynamics, media pressures, and the absence of ideological conviction conspire to produce leaders who are reactive rather than visionary. Leaders who dominate the political stage for a moment, only to leave behind little of consequence. The emphasis on personality over policy, marketing over meaning, has hollowed out leadership.

The focus here is not on individual failings, though there are plenty to consider. Instead, it's on structural forces that shape and constrain political leadership in the current era. Even the most capable political actors are operating within a system that rewards caution, punishes authenticity, and elevates spin above substance. In such an environment, the idea of building a legacy becomes not just difficult, it's actively discouraged.

In the sections that follow, I'll explore the transformation of political leadership from the Hawke and Keating years through to the revolving door of prime ministers that defined the past two decades. The comparison is telling. Where once leaders led, now they follow, using the tools of professional political practice when doing so. The result is a political class of tacticians, not statesmen.

The Revolving Door of Prime Ministers

Australia's recent political history reads like a case study in instability. Between 2007 and 2022, the country cycled through six prime ministers, with leadership changes often driven not by electoral defeat, but by internal party coups. Kevin Rudd, Julia Gillard, Tony Abbott, Malcolm Turnbull and Scott Morrison all assumed or lost the top job through intra-party manoeuvring. This churn reflects more than just personality clashes or factional rivalries. It marks a deeper transformation in the nature of political leadership, where longevity and legacy have been displaced by volatility and the short term.

The decline in leadership stability can be traced back to the end of John Howard's tenure. Love him or loathe him, Howard served as prime minister for over a decade, shaping the political landscape in his image. His successors have, by contrast, struggled to survive more than a single term, or even to complete one. The so-called "revolving door" of prime ministers has become a defining feature of federal politics, turning leadership into a precarious role rather than a position of sustained authority. And don't think that Anthony Albanese's successful re-election has broken this mirth. Rather, it may simply be the next step in the hollowing out of Australian politics, where a leader can win and avoid the churn by doing very little and standing for even less.

The leadership instability of the Rudd-Gillard-Rudd years set a precedent, but it wasn't isolated to Labor. The Liberals quickly adopted the same culture of internal contest. Abbott's shafting at the hands of Turnbull in 2015 mirrored the ruthless pragmatism of the Labor years.

And Turnbull's own removal and replacement by Morrison in 2018 confirmed that no prime minister could feel secure in the job. Internal polling, media sentiment, and factional pressure came to outweigh public mandates. It was politics in a permanent state of flux. This hasn't changed with Albanese's re-election either.

This cycle of instability bred a form of defensive leadership. Leaders governed not with a view to shaping the nation's future, but with a constant eye over their shoulders. The internal party room became the main threat to their survival. As a result, policy ambition was curtailed. Risks were avoided. The very idea of political courage, of embracing unpopular decisions for the longer-term good, became almost laughable in such an environment. The metric of success shifted from legacy to longevity. We now hear that openly sold as Albanese's contribution, despite him sitting on the progressive side of the ideological major party divide.

What made this all the more corrosive was the erosion of trust between leaders and their colleagues. Prime ministers no longer command loyalty simply by virtue of incumbency or electoral success. Instead, their authority is subject to constant negotiation. Factional leaders operate as powerbrokers, capable of toppling even sitting prime ministers. The rise of such internal kingmakers creates a new form of political calculus: one based less on performance in office, and more on factional arithmetic and behind-the-scenes manoeuvring. Albanese just happens to be pretty good at that.

The result has been a generation of leaders more focused on managing their colleagues than managing the country. With the party room transformed into a battlefield, prime ministers often retreated into narrow circles of advisers and loyalists. Decision-making became more centralised, more secretive, and more risk-averse. Ministers were sidelined, cabinet became a rubber stamp.

Political leadership, in this context, became not an opportunity to lead, but a constant struggle to survive.

None of the prime ministers between Howard and Albanese left a transformative imprint on the country, and Albanese doesn't look like doing so either. Some governed competently in parts, others disastrously, but few can lay claim to lasting reform. Rudd's National Broadband Network was partly dismantled. Gillard's carbon pricing scheme was scrapped. Abbott's agenda was largely obstructed or self-sabotaged. Turnbull's attempts at energy reform were thwarted by his own party, and he junked meaningful tax and federation white papers that Abbott had commissioned. Morrison's tenure was marked more by secrecy and crisis management than vision. The cycle of instability didn't just shorten the time leaders had in office, it undermined their capacity to build anything enduring within it.

Even when longevity returned, as with Morrison's full term (2019-2022) and now with Albanese's re-election, it has not been accompanied by substantial policy achievements. Instead, the leadership style remains insular and controlling, with a focus on managing perception rather than shaping policy direction. Longevity alone is no substitute for legacy. The Morrison government demonstrated that in abundance and the Albanese government is well on its way to doing the same.

The emergence of Anthony Albanese may signal a return to leadership stability, at least, but whether it also marks a return to purposeful leadership remains highly doubtful. The system itself, with its incentives for risk-aversion, its hyper-partisan media environment and its increasingly factionalised party structures, continues to constrain even well-intentioned leaders. Stability may be necessary for legacy, but it is not sufficient. Without the courage to pursue reform and the capacity to hold the party room together in its service, leadership remains a title, not a role.

Australia's revolving door of prime ministers has become more than a historical aberration. It reflects the deeper structural and cultural shifts that have hollowed out leadership itself. In the chapters that follow, we turn to the consequences of this evolution, not just for the leaders themselves, but for the nation they are meant to lead.

Power without Reform

The modern Australian prime minister is powerful but rarely transformative. The office still holds immense formal authority, yet the capacity to convert that power into lasting reform has steadily diminished. This is the paradox of contemporary leadership: prime ministers can dominate the political landscape, manipulate media narratives, and silence dissent within their own parties, yet leave behind little in the way of enduring policy achievements.

The result is a kind of executive emptiness: power exercised for survival. Part of this stems from the internal dynamics of party politics. Leadership contests are increasingly shaped by factional arithmetic, short-term polling, and media performance, not by policy platforms or ideological direction. Once in office, leaders often find themselves hemmed in by the very alliances that secured their elevation in the first place. They owe their position to factions, powerbrokers, and tactical alignments, not to a mandate for reform. This makes them naturally cautious. Reform invites controversy and controversy risks destabilisation. Destabilisation, as recent history has shown, often ends in political death.

The broader political ecosystem reinforces this caution. The Senate remains an unpredictable chamber, often controlled by micro-parties or populist independents. Negotiating reform becomes a process of dilution, more about appeasing gatekeepers than building consensus. Minority interests wield disproportionate power. Added to this is a risk-averse public service, politicised ministerial offices, and a media cycle that punishes complexity. It becomes all too clear why reformist leadership has become the exception rather than the rule.

Even when political capital exists, it is rarely spent. Leaders hoard authority, mindful of potential leadership challenges, wary of alienating key constituencies. In this context, the very language of reform has become degraded, only invoked for effect. Policy initiatives are framed in the language of transformation, but calibrated to offend no one. Ambition is replaced by performative governance: something must be seen to be done, even if nothing of substance changes.

The Rudd government, for all its initial energy, quickly succumbed to this syndrome. A sweeping reform agenda: the National Broadband Network, health reform and emissions trading, were all either stalled, abandoned or gutted in the face of political headwinds. Rudd's own leadership style exacerbated the problem: centralised, controlling and increasingly mistrusted by his colleagues. Rudd's eventual downfall came not because of failed reform, but because of how reform was pursued. It was top-down, often without consultation or coalition-building.

Gillard's tenure, while more consultative, was hampered by her minority government status and the toxic politics of the Rudd legacy. Her carbon pricing scheme, a genuine structural reform, was undermined both by external opposition and internal inconsistencies. The policy's substance was lost in the political warfare that engulfed it. Its eventual repeal under Abbott marked the end of serious climate reform for the better part of a decade.

Abbott promised to "stop the boats" and "axe the taxes", both on carbon and the mining industry. His signature Paid Parental Leave scheme, once hailed as a bold policy, was quietly abandoned when the going got tough. Abbott had a mandate but no real plan of action, and his aversion to compromise ensured that reform was sacrificed on the altar of ideological purity.

Turnbull's leadership embodied the reformer constrained. He had ideas, but no room to move. Hemmed in by his party's right flank and the ghosts of past leaders, Turnbull offered modest reforms to innovation and infrastructure, but failed to deliver on climate or energy, the issues that had once defined his political identity. His downfall was not about failure to reform, but failure to appease those within his party who feared reform. In the end he achieved neither.

Morrison, by contrast, never pretended to be a reformer. His leadership style was managerial, reactive, and deliberately narrow in ambition. Even when faced with crises that might have spurred structural change (the bushfires and the pandemic) Morrison's response was tactical, not transformational. His political success, paradoxically, lay in doing as little as possible while appearing busy.

This trend towards power without reform has broader implications. It feeds public cynicism, erodes trust in institutions, and entrenches the perception that politics is disconnected from the real challenges facing the country. When governments fail to act on housing affordability, tax reform, climate change, or productivity because the politics is too hard, democracy suffers. The gap between what is possible and what is pursued widens, and into that void steps disillusionment, populism and voter disengagement.

If legacy is built on reform, then Australia's recent crop of prime ministers has little to show for their time in office. Their names are remembered more for the drama of their ascents and downfalls than for any enduring national transformation. Leadership, in this model, is an office to be held, not a platform to effect change.

The Politics of Cosmetic Change

In contemporary Australian politics, reform is often framed as a communications exercise rather than a policy imperative. Politicians seek to appear as reformers without taking the political risks that genuine reform entails. The result is a culture of symbolic gestures: legislative tweaks, white papers that go nowhere, or grand announcements unaccompanied by legislative follow-through.

The Rudd-Gillard years provide an illustrative case study. There were genuine ambitions to tackle long-term challenges, think health reform, education funding or carbon pricing. But those ambitions were routinely stymied by political caution, internal division, and external opposition. The mining tax was compromised, the carbon tax became a political liability, and education reforms like Gonski were left underfunded or sidelined. Even well-intentioned reforms were strangled by the politics of pragmatism.

On the Coalition side, the problem has often been one of rhetorical reformism with no substantive follow-through. Tony Abbott promised to be an "infrastructure prime minister," but underinvested in major nation-building projects. Scott Morrison declared a commitment to energy security but offered no clear path forward on climate change. The rhetoric of reform was decoupled from the hard graft of policy work. Instead, the focus was on slogans and short-term advantage.

This performative approach to reform fosters a broader cynicism in the electorate. When voters see successive governments promise change without delivering it, trust in institutions erodes. It's not merely that governments fail to act, it's that they pretend to act while entrenching stasis. This deepens disengagement and further diminishes the appetite for future reforms. Why believe the next promise when the last one led nowhere?

Consultants and political advisers have played a growing role in facilitating this dynamic. Reforms are often scoped by external firms more skilled in branding than policy design. Announcements are stage-managed to suit media cycles. Ministers become performers rather than policymakers. The substance of reform is outsourced or neglected, as political calculations drive every decision.

There is also a growing reluctance to challenge powerful interests. From tax reform to housing affordability to media regulation, governments shy away from difficult fights. The lobbying power of the fossil fuel industry, the financial sector, or property developers ensures that any reform touching their interests is carefully neutered. In a democracy where influence is concentrated and political donations remain opaque, courage is the first casualty.

Even reform processes themselves have been undermined. Where once royal commissions or major inquiries were vehicles for confronting hard truths, they now often serve political ends. Terms of reference are tightly drawn, findings selectively implemented, and timelines manipulated for electoral gain. The appearance of reform is more valuable than the reality.

This is not to say that all reform is impossible. Periodically, breakthrough moments occur, often when political will converges with public demand and institutional capacity. But those moments have become rare. More often, the prevailing trend is one of dilution: ambition blunted by calculation. And over time, the accumulation of missed opportunities hollows out the very concept of reform.

The result is a polity that talks about reform incessantly but does little to realise it. This has profound implications. It means structural challenges, from productivity stagnation to intergenerational inequality, are largely left unaddressed. It means public institutions struggle to modernise. And it means the public grows ever more cynical about the capacity of politics to deliver.

A Retreat from Principle leaving Reform in Name only

One of the defining features of Australia's modern political culture is the almost complete retreat from principle. In its place is a form of political management that privileges pragmatism, triangulation and tactical calculations. Values are selectively deployed, usually summoned for rhetorical effect then abandoned when inconvenient. What remains is a hollow politics, and leadership is indistinguishable from opportunism.

This retreat is the product of decades of political evolution, during which parties increasingly viewed electoral success as an end in itself. Policy platforms were shaped less by ideology than by market research. The focus of party leaders shifted from articulating a vision to avoiding controversy. Tough reforms were shelved; principled stands were cast as liabilities. In this environment, courage was redefined as recklessness.

Nowhere has this been more evident than in debates over climate change. Despite overwhelming scientific consensus and public support for action, successive Australian governments have treated climate policy as a political liability rather than a moral imperative. Leaders have trimmed their sails to prevailing winds, abandoned policy frameworks midstream, and demonised opponents rather than building consensus. Both major parties have done it in their own ways. The result is paralysis.

The retreat from principle has profound implications for democracy. It leaves the electorate with little sense of what political leaders actually stand for. Policy distinctions blur. Elections become contests between personalities rather than ideas. Voter disengagement rises, and cynicism deepens. When politics becomes unmoored from principle, trust becomes the collateral damage.

It also affects the quality of governance. Without a clear philosophical foundation, governments drift from one crisis to the next. Perhaps most disturbingly, the abandonment of principle hollows out the very purpose of politics. If the goal is merely to win and hold power then politics becomes a transactional game rather than a public vocation. It becomes harder to inspire, to mobilise or to lead.

In contemporary Australian politics, reform is often discussed in lofty terms. Yet far too often, what is labelled "reform" amounts to little more than technocratic tinkering or politically expedient adjustments. Structural change is avoided, difficult decisions are postponed, and systemic challenges are met with cosmetic solutions. The language of reform remains, but its meaning has been diluted.

This is not merely a matter of rhetorical inflation. There has been a shift in how reform is conceived: from a bold reimagining of public policy in service of long-term national interest to a risk-managed process shaped by short-term political calculation. The Hawke and Keating governments set a high watermark in this regard. They undertook politically painful reforms not because they were popular, but because they were necessary. Those reforms reshaped Australia's economic landscape and are now widely credited with underpinning decades of growth.

Today, such courage in politics is largely absent. Governments prefer to commission reviews rather than commit to change even when that's what the commissioned review calls for. Reform agendas are announced but rarely implemented. When they are, they tend to be narrow in scope and negotiated down to the least controversial denominator. Bipartisanship is no longer sought, let alone achieved. Instead, reform is framed as a contest, just another front in the political battle. Such framing ensures that even modest proposals can be weaponised by the opposition and abandoned by those who floated them.

This is particularly evident in areas like tax policy. Everyone agrees the system is outdated: riddled with inefficiencies, distortions, and unsustainable concessions. Yet proposals for genuine reform, such as negative gearing changes or a broadening of the GST, are quickly torpedoed by scare campaigns or shelved due to electoral risk.

Even when genuine reform proposals are put forward, they are rarely communicated effectively. Governments fail to build the case, explain the rationale, or create a sense of shared purpose. Reform becomes a transactional offer, not a transformative project. There is little effort to rally public support or frame reform as a national endeavour. Without leadership and persuasion reforms lack legitimacy, and without legitimacy they are vulnerable to reversal.

The danger of this dynamic is not just policy inertia. It is a deeper erosion of public faith in the political system's capacity to evolve. When governments are seen as incapable of tackling hard problems, voters turn to protest parties or disengage altogether. Reform becomes synonymous with disruption, not improvement. Trust in the process collapses.

Chapter 8
THE PARTY'S OVER?

Australia's major political parties once played a defining role in the nation's democratic life. They were vehicles for ideological contest, communities of civic engagement, and the institutional backbone of representative government. But in recent decades, their vitality has drained away. Membership has collapsed, local branches have withered and internal democracy has atrophied. The parties remain as hollowed-out shells now controlled by professionalised careerists.

It reflects the dominance of marketing over messaging and the drift towards managerialism. Parties have become instruments of career advancement rather than forums for debate. Their focus has narrowed to tactical manoeuvring and factional advantage, with little space for the kind of open deliberation that once sustained ideological zeal.

This chapter explores how party structures have been weakened, often by those who lead them. It examines the fading of branch life, the rise of factional powerbrokers, the replacement of grassroots activism with outsourced campaigning and the loss of principle in favour of pragmatism. In a democracy where parties still serve as the gatekeepers to political office, their decline carries serious consequences. Not just for those within them, but for the quality of governance itself.

The party system hasn't collapsed, but it has curdled, and the implications for Australian democracy are only just beginning to show.

From Mass Membership to Hollow Shells

There was a time when political parties in Australia were deeply embedded in the social and civic fabric of the nation. They served not merely as electoral machines but as institutions of political education, mobilisation, and representation. Local branches were vibrant centres of ideological debate, policy discussion, and community organisation. They provided forums where members shaped platforms, selected candidates, and engaged in the life of the party between elections. To be a party member was to participate in a broader national conversation, giving members a sense of ownership over the democratic process, rather than passive spectatorship.

That era has long since passed. Today, Australia's major political parties are organisational husks of what they once were. Mass participation has been replaced by professionalisation. Grassroots engagement has given way to campaign coordination. The Labor Party, once rooted in union membership and local activism, has seen a steady attrition of rank-and-file involvement. The Liberal Party, historically reliant on civic-minded volunteers and community-based branches, has arguably fared worse. Its base has narrowed, and its structures have become increasingly top-down. Almost a return to the cadre model of party. In both cases, political parties now operate more like political franchises, managed from the centre, concerned primarily with brand protection and electoral success.

This collapse in membership isn't just a structural issue; it speaks to a broader decline in political meaning. Citizens are less inclined to join parties because the benefits of membership have become unclear. There is little sense that involvement offers genuine influence over decision-making or policy direction. Instead, members often find themselves relegated to the margins, expected to do some groundwork during election campaigns but excluded from substantive input the rest of the time. The internal life of parties has become dominated by factional interests, pre-parliamentary careerists, and apparatchiks whose primary goal is often personal advancement rather than public service.

The implications are far-reaching. First, the disintegration of mass membership has undermined the connective tissue between elected representatives and the communities they serve. Parties without members are parties without roots, organisations that drift toward technocracy or populism depending on the political winds. Voters become targets of marketing campaigns rather than participants in democratic deliberation. Policy formation, once enriched by internal contestation and bottom-up contributions, now flows downward from leaders, informed more by polling and focus groups than ideological commitments or member consensus.

Second, this hollowing out has concentrated power in the hands of a small political elite: party executives, parliamentary leaders, and factional powerbrokers. Preselections, once contested vigorously at the local level, are now often orchestrated from above. In the ALP, community preselections have been introduced in some areas, but they remain the exception rather than the rule and are frequently subjected to behind-the-scenes manipulation. The Liberal Party's experiments with member plebiscites have similarly failed to curb the dominance of factional heavyweights. Instead of invigorating party life, these measures have often reinforced cynicism about how decisions are really made.

This centralisation of control has also narrowed the pipeline into politics. With fewer genuine members and tighter control over preselections, candidates are increasingly drawn from a narrow class of political operatives, staffers and insiders. Rather than community leaders or professionals bringing external experience into parliament, parties now select individuals who have risen through internal networks. People fluent in the language of factional loyalty, media spin, and tactical manoeuvring. The result is a growing detachment between the political class and the electorate, a sense that politicians speak a language and occupy a world increasingly foreign to those they claim to represent.

The digital era was once seen as a potential solution to this decline, a means of reviving political engagement through new forms of participation. But while social media and online platforms have offered parties tools for outreach and mobilisation, they have not reversed the long-term disengagement. In fact, they have arguably exacerbated it. Online engagement has tended to substitute for meaningful involvement rather than complement it. The party's message is broadcast, not debated. Internal democracy has atrophied in the face of carefully managed communications strategies and tightly controlled narratives.

This transformation has rendered political parties increasingly brittle. Without the legitimacy and dynamism that comes from mass membership, they struggle to renew themselves or respond to shifting social demands. They lack the internal contest that once drove policy innovation and ideological clarity. They are more vulnerable to external capture, whether by wealthy donors, lobbyists or narrow self-interested factions. And they are less equipped to weather public discontent, as voters turn to independents, protest candidates or minor parties that promise authenticity, however illusory.

The decline of party membership also has implications for governance. Parties that are disconnected from society are more likely to govern with a narrow focus, appealing to base constituencies or median voters rather than the broader public interest. Their leaders become risk-averse, obsessed with short-term media cycles and electoral tactics. Policy ambition is traded for political survival.

Democratic participation becomes a periodic event rather than an ongoing process embedded in civic institutions.

Ultimately, the shift from mass membership to hollow shells marks a fundamental change in how Australian democracy functions. It represents a retreat from collective political identity, a weakening of the institutions that once mediated between citizens and the state. Voter dealignment has been happening for many years. The consequences are already visible: lower trust in politicians, greater volatility in electoral outcomes, and the rise of anti-establishment sentiment. Parties, once engines of democratic participation, now resemble marketing firms more than movements, chasing votes rather than convictions.

The Rise of the Political Class

As party membership declined and grassroots influence waned, a new type of political operator emerged, one less tethered to community engagement and more embedded in the machinery of politics itself. The rise of the political class has fundamentally altered the character of Australian political parties. These are not public servants in the traditional sense, nor are they ideological warriors fighting for big ideas. Instead, they are careerists, highly attuned to the rhythm of Canberra, fluent in media management and deeply invested in maintaining their proximity to power.

This political class is often born and bred within the system. Many of today's federal MPs began as student politicians, parliamentary staffers, or union officials. They graduated not from public service or business, but from the internal hierarchies of their respective parties. Their ascent is marked less by real-world experience than by loyalty to factional networks and success in navigating internal contests. The result is a self-perpetuating elite, insiders selecting and promoting other insiders, with little incentive to look beyond the political bubble.

These individuals are not without talent. Many of them could have had successful careers in other professions had that been where their interest lay. But having decided that a political career was what they wanted, they gave up on chasing success elsewhere and focused on employment within the political bubble, stifling their knowledge and breadth in other areas which was what previously served the parliament so well. That diversity of pre-parliamentary backgrounds is no more.

The professionalisation of politics has had profound effects on how parties operate. Where once candidates were drawn from a broad cross-section of society (local businesspeople, teachers, doctors, farmers, you name it) today's political aspirants are disproportionately drawn from a narrow, ideologically homogeneous pool. This narrowing of background and perspective not only erodes the diversity of parliamentary representation, it reinforces a technocratic approach to governance: politics as a job, not a calling.

In practice, this means fewer elected representatives bring lived experience of the communities they represent. Their connection to the electorate is mediated through polling, media briefings and campaign advisers rather than through direct engagement or personal insight. This detachment is evident in the language of politics: managerial, scripted, and heavily focus-grouped. And in the reluctance to take principled stands that might conflict with electoral calculations.

This culture encourages conformity over conviction. Challengers of the status quo, whether within parties or outside them, are marginalised. Dissent becomes dangerous, innovation is seen as risky, and ambition is funnelled into the tactical, not the transformational. The political class is adept at managing narratives, but far less comfortable engaging with competing ideas. As a result, parties become more homogeneous, less intellectually vibrant, and more risk-averse.

Voters can sense the difference. They see through the scripted talking points, the stage-managed appearances, and the evasive interviews. They recognise when their representatives are playing a role rather than representing a view. Increasingly they disengage, not out of apathy, but out of disillusionment with a political system that seems less interested in solving problems than simply managing perceptions.

This erosion of authenticity lies at the heart of the public's growing disaffection with politics. It's not just that the major parties have fewer members or stale platforms, it's that the people running them often seem more loyal to the party machine than to any broader cause. The political class has become its own constituency: insular, self-referential and increasingly out of step with the country it purports to govern.

Factionalism over Function

Factions were once seen as a necessary, even healthy, part of political life. In the Labor Party, they reflected ideological and industrial divisions: left and right, unions and members, reformists and traditionalists. In the Liberal Party, groupings were looser, more personality-driven, but still broadly reflective of philosophical differences. They preferred to call their groupings "tendencies". But in today's hollowed-out party structures, factionalism has shifted from ideological contest to career management. The purpose of factions is no longer to shape the direction of the party, it's to secure influence within it.

This shift has had corrosive effects. Power is concentrated in the hands of factional warlords who can deliver numbers at party conferences, dominate preselection processes and dictate internal appointments. Merit and performance matter less than loyalty and alignment. In some cases, candidates are installed despite local opposition. In others, talented outsiders are actively discouraged from standing, because they pose a threat to factional equilibrium.

The consequence is a party culture that prioritises control over contribution. Ideas become secondary to allegiances. Policy debates are stifled if they risk opening new lines of division or challenging the dominant faction's authority. Even in government, factional leaders continue to wield influence behind the scenes, pressuring ministers, allocating resources, and shaping Cabinet appointments based on factional arithmetic rather than national interest.

For the Liberals, factionalism has become especially toxic. The party's long-standing divisions between moderates, conservatives, and libertarians have hardened into permanent, zero-sum contests. In some state branches (New South Wales most notably) the party has been paralysed by infighting, legal challenges, and public brawls over candidate selection. This factionalism has not only weakened the party's electoral prospects but undermined public confidence in its capacity to govern coherently.

Labor's factionalism is more institutionalised, a by-product of its union affiliations and internal rules. Deals are often stitched up behind closed doors, limiting transparency and accountability. Promising voices from outside the factional system struggle to gain traction, while long-term loyalty to a faction can act as a shield against underperformance or controversy. The recent history of federal Labor shows a party adept at managing its internal coalitions but cautious, even timid, in pursuing reform.

What gets lost in all of this is the public interest. When parties are consumed by internal jockeying, they lose sight of their broader purpose. Parliament becomes a venue for settling scores, not debating ideas. Policy becomes a tool of factional compromise, not a blueprint for progress. Voters rightly grow cynical, not just about the individuals involved, but about the legitimacy of the system itself.

Factionalism is not new, but in an era where parties are already weakened by low membership, shallow engagement and a professional political class, it becomes particularly destructive. It hollows out internal democracy, alienates potential recruits and fosters a culture of mediocrity. And perhaps most damaging of all it entrenches a mindset where loyalty to the faction outweighs responsibility to the public.

The Decline of Internal Participation

At the heart of any democratic party should be the active engagement of its members. Branch meetings, policy forums, preselections, and party conferences once provided avenues for rank-and-file participation, giving members a real voice in shaping the direction and leadership of their party. But today these mechanisms exist largely in name only. Internal democracy has been systematically weakened, sidelined by centralised power structures, and rendered performative rather than participatory. Don't let the trinket of members having a say in electing the parliamentary leader of the Labor Party gloss over the real decline in a role for members in party and policy activities.

The causes are varied but reinforcing. As membership numbers have collapsed, the remaining participants are disproportionately factional operatives or politically ambitious insiders. This has created a feedback loop: genuine members drop out as their influence wanes, while the party becomes more insular and unrepresentative. The infrastructure of participation (local branches, policy committees and conferences) still exists, but their function is increasingly symbolic. Real decisions are made elsewhere.

Preselection contests are perhaps the clearest example. In both major parties, they have become battlegrounds for factional dominance rather than democratic deliberation. In Labor, union affiliates wield disproportionate power, often outvoting rank-and-file members.

In the Liberal Party, party executives have intervened repeatedly to override local outcomes, sometimes parachuting in candidates, other times cancelling votes entirely. Labor has done that too in recent years, at the direction of the Prime Minister no less. Promises of member empowerment are frequently abandoned when they threaten the preferences of powerbrokers or the leader.

The decline of internal democracy also manifests in policy development. In theory, parties are meant to be sites of ideological debate: laboratories of ideas, informed by member input and collective discussion. In practice, policy platforms are often devised by small inner circles, ratified without meaningful debate and sold to the base as fait accompli. Members might be consulted after the fact, but rarely are they involved in shaping the vision from the ground up.

This centralisation reflects the broader professionalisation of political parties. Modern campaign strategies prioritise message discipline, brand control and electoral management, all of which are seen as incompatible with bottom-up deliberation. Rank-and-file participation is treated as a risk rather than a resource. Dissent is discouraged, complexity avoided and spontaneity eliminated. The result is a party culture that values compliance over creativity and loyalty over leadership.

There are, of course, exceptions. Some state branches have trialled more inclusive preselection models. Community forums and online consultations have been used, sporadically, to gather wider input. But these initiatives are often short-lived or selectively applied. The structural incentives still favour central control. And without meaningful reform, such experiments risk becoming window dressing. Gestures of inclusion that change little in practice.

The long-term consequences are profound. As parties become less internally democratic, they lose their legitimacy as vehicles of democratic expression. The gap between political elites and ordinary citizens therefore widens. Voters become consumers of politics rather than participants in it. And parties themselves are weakened, not just electorally, but institutionally.

Parties without Purpose

At the heart of the hollowing out of Australia's political parties lies a deeper malaise: the loss of purpose. Once grounded in ideological commitments — Labor in the labour movement and social democracy, the Liberals in liberal-conservatism and free enterprise — today's major parties increasingly operate as brands rather than movements. Their core business has become electoral success, not policy reform or societal vision. They contest power, but often without a clear sense of what to do with it.

This drift didn't happen overnight. As parties professionalised and centralised, their policy platforms became more reactive, shaped by polling and focus groups rather than long-held principles or grassroots demands. The desire to avoid alienating swinging voters led to a kind of ideological convergence, particularly on economic policy. Labor embraced market liberalisation under Hawke and Keating; the Liberals under Howard and beyond, conceded ground on social policy to broaden appeal. The result has been a narrowing of the political spectrum, with both sides pursuing versions of managerial centrism.

In this environment, conviction politics is not just rare, it's now actively discouraged. Leaders who articulate a clear philosophical vision risk being painted as ideologues or out of touch. Ambitious reform is shelved in favour of incrementalism. Complex problems are reduced to slogans. Voters sense the vacuity, which is why increasing numbers turn to independents, minor parties or simply disengage entirely. They see the major parties not as vehicles for change, but as hollow institutions obsessed with optics.

This lack of purpose is reinforced by the parties' internal cultures. When power is concentrated among factional elites and political professionals, policy debate becomes secondary to career advancement and internal positioning. Parliamentary party rooms rarely engage in genuine contestation of ideas. Instead, policy is dictated from the leader's office or shaped by factional deals. Even where there is an internal appetite for reform, it is often stifled by the fear of electoral backlash or donor displeasure.

The media environment further entrenches this shallowness of course. The dominance of the daily news cycle, the rise of social media and the obsession with "gotcha" journalism all reward risk-averse politics. Leaders are trained to stay on message, avoid details and speak in pre-tested soundbites. The consequence is not just bland politics, it's an erosion of the very idea that politics can be a contest of values and vision.

If the parties themselves can't articulate a purpose beyond winning, they shouldn't be surprised when voters turn away in disgust. Politics, at its best, is about building coalitions around ideas, offering competing visions for the future, and engaging citizens in democratic life. When parties become little more than campaign machines, they lose that function. They remain powerful, but not persuasive. They endure, but they no longer inspire. That is the true danger of a hollow party system.

Chapter 9

BUREAUCRACY WITHOUT BACKBONE

The public service has long been described as the engine room of government. An institution designed to provide continuity, expertise, and impartial advice regardless of which political party holds office. But in contemporary Australian politics, that ideal has been eroded. What remains is a bureaucracy increasingly shaped by political considerations and sidelined in favour of short-term needs.

Over time, the independence of the public service has been compromised. Ministers now expect not just responsiveness but alignment, and senior public servants often deliver it, either out of careerist instincts or political expediency. The revolving door between politics and consulting firms has further blurred the lines of accountability. Once expected to offer "frank and fearless advice," bureaucrats now navigate a culture in which challenging the minister can mean professional exile.

At the same time, the capacity of the public service has been hollowed out. As discussed earlier, the rise of private consultants has sapped departments of expertise, initiative and institutional memory. Public servants are increasingly relegated to contract managers, overseeing outsourced work rather than shaping policy themselves. This is not just a question of inefficiency or waste, though both are real concerns. It speaks to a deeper loss of public purpose, a drift away from the core responsibilities that once defined the bureaucracy's role in democratic life. The result is a system of governance that is reactive rather than strategic.

This chapter examines the decline of Australia's once-robust public service. It is not simply a story of underfunding or administrative drift. It is about the loss of an ethos: that public administration is a vocation rooted in service to the common good, not just a tool for political management. In what follows, I unpack the drivers of this shift and its consequences.

From Stewardship to Service Delivery

For much of the twentieth century, Australia's public service was characterised by its role as steward of the national interest. It was built on the premise that good governance required continuity, institutional knowledge and impartial advice: Qualities that positioned the bureaucracy as a critical force behind stable democratic government. But in recent decades, the idea of the public sector as a steward has been replaced with a far narrower conception: that of a service provider, focused on efficiency, delivery and customer satisfaction. What was once an institution of policy depth and civic duty is now expected to operate more like a private enterprise, responsive to ministerial whims, judged by performance metrics, and increasingly divorced from its former role in shaping long-term public policy.

This shift began in earnest during the Hawke-Keating years, with the embrace of New Public Management and the framing of government services through the language of markets. Bureaucrats became managers, departments became agencies, and the language of stewardship (of careful deliberative policy) gave way to terms like outputs, KPIs, and cost-efficiency. While intended to improve public sector responsiveness, the reforms also eroded something essential: the idea that the public service should offer not just execution, but guidance. It created a culture more focused on deliverables than on direction, one in which long-term thinking was too easily sacrificed at the altar of short-term performance.

The consequences of this shift were not immediately obvious. Indeed, in the early years, performance seemed to improve in some areas. Government departments adopted clearer planning frameworks, timelines tightened, and service delivery — particularly in areas like licensing, taxation and social services — became more customer-focused. But as the reforms deepened, the risks became clearer. The pursuit of efficiencies often came at the expense of quality. Departments were increasingly reluctant to challenge ministers, preferring to over-deliver rather than offer difficult advice. The language of public good was replaced by that of transactional compliance. The service could still execute policy — but it was losing the ability to shape it. The rise and rise of political staffing within ministerial offices contributed to this.

Where once policy teams would develop expertise over decades, capable of drawing on institutional memory and comparative analysis, the public service started to become more transitory. Career progression often required moving quickly between portfolios, limiting the opportunity for deep subject-matter expertise. Combined with budgetary pressures and job insecurity, especially at middle and senior management levels, the result was a bureaucracy less confident in its own policy voice. Many departments outsourced that role altogether, turning to consultants, lobbyists or politically appointed staffers to do work that had traditionally been done internally.

Politicians, for their part, increasingly saw the public service as a tool to be used rather than a partner to be respected. Ministers preferred loyalty over frankness, speed over nuance. Departments learned to second-guess political preferences, often pre-emptively sanitising policy options to avoid confrontation or embarrassment. The cultural shift was subtle but significant: once prized for their independence and rigour, public servants began to be valued for their compliance and discretion. A service designed to stand the test of time had become one shaped by the news cycle.

Even rhetorical shifts captured the change. Governments began referring to "clients" and "customers" rather than citizens or constituents. The language of service delivery, borrowed from the private sector, became ubiquitous. Yet the public sector is not a business, and its goals cannot be reduced to market transactions. It must balance competing interests, manage limited resources, and deliver not just services but social cohesion, equity, and accountability. The conversion of the bureaucracy into a customer service organisation has diminished its capacity to fulfil those broader, more complex roles.

None of this is to argue for a return to a pre-reform era of slow-moving, unaccountable bureaucracy. Efficiency and responsiveness matter. But the pendulum has swung too far away from stewardship, away from strategic policy capacity and away from a public service capable of acting as a genuine partner in government. The hollowing out of its advisory role has weakened governance and contributed to a broader erosion of public trust in the political system. Restoring balance means more than reshaping organisational charts, it requires a cultural shift back towards valuing public service not just for what it delivers but for how it thinks.

The Politicisation of Advice

The tradition of "frank and fearless" advice from the public service to ministers was once a defining feature of Australian governance. Senior public servants were expected to challenge, question, and interrogate policy proposals, even when they clashed with the preferences of their political masters. Their duty was to the public interest, not the party in power. But over the past two decades, that culture has eroded. Ministers no longer expect independent analysis, they prefer acquiescence. The result is a politicised bureaucracy where advice is shaped not by evidence or long-term thinking, but by what ministers want to hear.

This shift has not occurred by accident. Governments of both persuasions have sought greater control over the machinery of government, seeing the public service not as a source of wisdom but as an extension of their political agenda. Departmental secretaries are now selected less for their policy credentials than for their perceived loyalty or pliability. Under the Morrison government, this trend was particularly pronounced: secretaries were moved in and out of key roles with little explanation, and senior appointments often seemed more about ideological alignment than merit.

The presence of ministerial advisers has also helped drive this politicisation, as alluded to already. Advisers are political operatives, not public servants. Their role is to serve the minister's political interests, which often means sidelining bureaucratic advice that doesn't align with the desired message or outcome. Over time public servants have internalised this dynamic, learning to second-guess what ministers want. Rather than present a range of options, they present the option they think is most likely to be accepted. Innovation and dissent are discouraged. Caution becomes the norm.

This change is compounded by the revolving door between politics and the public service. Former ministerial staffers are all too freely parachuted into senior bureaucratic positions, while ex-public servants take up roles in lobbying firms or ministerial offices. The lines between neutral administration and political advocacy have blurred. It's no longer clear where politics ends and the public service begins. And in that confusion, it is the independence of public administration that suffers.

Political staffers have always wielded influence, but their dominance is now institutionalised. They act as gatekeepers, controlling the flow of information to and from ministers, deciding who gets access and what advice is seen. This creates a culture of insulation: ministers are protected from uncomfortable truths, and public servants are discouraged from raising inconvenient facts. The machinery of government becomes less about governing and more about managing optics.

This culture of politicised advice has led to real-world consequences. Major policy failures, such as the bungled rollout of the NDIS to the debacle of Robodebt, were not simply implementation errors. They reflected a deeper failure of governance: the suppression of expert advice, the prioritisation of spin over substance and a reluctance to challenge political orthodoxy. When public servants are incentivised to say what ministers want to hear, rather than what they need to know, bad outcomes become more likely.

The Robodebt Royal Commission exposed precisely this breakdown. Senior bureaucrats failed to push back against an unlawful scheme that affected hundreds of thousands of Australians. Internal concerns were downplayed, legal advice ignored, and accountability diluted. The public service became an enabler of executive overreach rather than a check on it. And when things unravelled, the political class was quick to deflect blame back onto the bureaucracy it had neutered.

This culture is reinforced by performance management systems that reward obedience and penalise dissent. Career advancement in the public service increasingly hinges on one's ability to navigate the political preferences of the day rather than demonstrate independent judgement or long-term thinking. Public servants know that challenging ministers or pushing unpopular advice can be career-limiting.

All of this contributes to a hollowing out of the public service's purpose. Rather than be the stewards of good governance, departments become service delivery agencies focused on implementing government policy, however flawed it might be. Their role is reactive, not proactive. Strategic policy units are sidelined or dismantled altogether. And the idea that public servants might shape national direction becomes quaint, even subversive.

There are, of course, still public servants who embody the best traditions of the profession. But they work in an environment that does not reward (and often actively punishes) those traditions. The political tail now wags the bureaucratic dog, and the consequence is a system of government less capable of solving complex problems.

The broader effect is corrosive. A politicised public service undermines trust in government. It contributes to the perception that decisions are driven by politics, not evidence. And it leaves citizens with the sense that the system is rigged. That even those charged with offering neutral, professional advice are just another arm of the political machine.

Restoring the independence and integrity of the public service will require more than structural reforms. It will demand a cultural shift, one that values courage over compliance and stewardship over subservience. Until that happens, the politicisation of advice will continue to weaken Australia's capacity to govern effectively.

Accountability in Retreat

Accountability in Australian public administration has become a hollow ritual, observed in form but not in substance. Ministers still front up to Question Time, committees still convene, and annual reports still get tabled. But behind these formalities, the machinery of scrutiny has weakened. The public service, once a conduit for transparency and institutional memory, has become increasingly opaque, shielded by layers of political management and selective disclosure. You only have to look at the administration of Freedom Of Information (FOI) requests. What we are left with is a culture where plausible deniability is more prized than performance and transparency, and where avoiding blame has become the dominant logic of governance.

One of the clearest manifestations of this trend is the treatment of ministerial responsibility. Once a cornerstone of Westminster-style democracy, the principle has eroded to the point of farce. Ministers routinely preside over significant administrative failures without resigning or accepting culpability. When scandals erupt, be it Robodebt, sports rorts or mismanaged procurements, the instinct is not contrition but obfuscation. Blame is shifted down the chain, often to departmental officials or conveniently vague "process failures." Ministers often avoid scrutiny by invoking confidentiality, blaming predecessors or hiding behind departmental advice.

Parliamentary scrutiny has not kept pace with the need for genuine accountability. Committees, once robust forums for interrogation, are often neutered by partisan control, ministerial stonewalling or pathetic grandstanding by committee members unqualified for the oversight tasks they are given. Witnesses dodge questions, documents are withheld and politically sensitive topics are redirected or delayed. Senate estimates hearings (once a powerful tool of oversight) have too often become mere theatre rather than a mechanism for truth-seeking. Public servants are coached before appearing, by their departmental media teams which aren't small. Answers are thus rehearsed and sanitised. Ministers selectively appear or delegate appearances, and answers are increasingly filtered through talking points.

This culture of avoidance has been compounded by changes in

information management. The use of private messaging apps for government business, delays in fulfilling FOI requests, and the growth of "cabinet-in-confidence" exemptions all serve to insulate decision-makers from scrutiny. The net effect is a public that is kept in the dark about how and why key decisions are made. Transparency is increasingly treated as an inconvenience rather than a democratic obligation.

Meanwhile, the lines of accountability between ministers and the public service have blurred. Senior public servants are no longer insulated from political pressures. Many are effectively co-opted into the government's political machinery. In some cases, they have become defenders of questionable conduct, issuing statements or running interference to shield ministers from fallout. Rather than upholding public interest, the incentive has shifted toward maintaining favour with political masters. This dynamic is exacerbated by the increasing number of fixed-term contracts for senior officials, making job security contingent on political loyalty rather than professional merit.

Media scrutiny, once a powerful external check, has been blunted. As will be detailed in the next chapter, the decline of investigative journalism, the growth of media management techniques, and the increasing complexity of government decision-making have all made it easier for serious missteps to go unexamined or be spun into non-events. The 24-hour news cycle, far from enhancing public oversight, has shortened political memories, allowing scandals to be survived through attrition rather than accountability.

The cumulative effect of these changes is a system where the incentives to govern responsibly have weakened. When failures carry limited consequences, when scrutiny can be managed, and when truth can be delayed or buried, the quality of governance inevitably suffers. The public sees the erosion of accountability, and trust in institutions continues to decline.

Fixing this requires more than procedural tweaks. It demands a cultural shift to support a reinvigoration of ministerial standards, a recommitment to transparency, and a strengthening of the institutional guardrails that protect against excess. It also requires a political class that recognises the value of being answerable to parliament as well as the broader public.

Public Sector in Name Only

In modern Australia, the public sector retains its name but has lost much of its original essence. It still occupies office buildings in Canberra, still administers programmes, and still submits departmental briefs for Minister's to consider. But the defining features that once made it a genuine public service — independence, expertise, institutional continuity — have steadily eroded. What remains is a workforce that has lost what it once had.

This isn't a critique of individual public servants. Many remain committed to the public good and carry out their responsibilities with professionalism and care. The issue lies in the structures they work within and the expectations imposed upon them. The transformation of the service into a managerial apparatus, tasked with executing political instructions rather than helping to shape them into good public policy ideas, has created a system that looks like a public sector but behaves increasingly like an arm of the government of the day.

The shift from stewardship to service delivery paved the way for this outcome. Once the public service was expected to be a custodian of institutional memory and a source of long-term policy development. It was staffed by career professionals whose tenure provided both continuity and ballast. Today the emphasis on managerial efficiency and outsourcing has diminished its capacity to act as a genuine repository of knowledge or independent policy thinking.

This has led to a creeping confusion about what the public service is for. Is it a neutral institution providing advice irrespective of a government's party political stripes? Or is it a delivery mechanism for whatever agenda the government of the day wishes to implement? The answer, in practice, has tilted firmly towards the latter. Departments are evaluated not on their stewardship or foresight, but on how efficiently they carry out instructions. Innovation is welcomed only when it aligns with ministerial preferences. Deviations from the script are discouraged.

The rise of short-term contracts and political appointments to senior public service roles has compounded the problem. Secretaries and senior executives are expected to be 'responsive', a euphemism for loyal. Those who fall out of favour, even for defending basic principles of public administration, can find themselves swiftly replaced. This undermines both morale and institutional independence. Over time, it creates a culture where ambition is tempered by caution, and candour is lost.

Moreover, the language used to describe the public service has changed. Ministers now speak of "government services" rather than "public administration". Citizens are "clients" or "customers". Policies are "products". Departments are "delivery arms". This corporate lexicon is not merely cosmetic. It reflects and reinforces a profound reimagining of what the public sector is. The language of marketing and efficiency has displaced the language of duty and stewardship. And with that, the ethos of the public service has been quietly transformed.

The cumulative effect is that the public sector, while still publicly funded and nominally impartial, operates increasingly like a quasi-political entity, one that serves political ends rather than democratic principles. Its legitimacy no longer flows from its institutional standing or public trust, but from its proximity to ministerial power. It has become a servant not of the people but of the government.

The Australian public service retains the symbols and rituals of an impartial institution, but its operating reality is quite different. Its culture is reactive, its independence compromised and its expertise underutilised and arguably now underdone. This is not an accidental outcome. It is the result of sustained political choices: to centralise power, to prize loyalty over merit, and to reframe governance through a commercial lens. The consequences are profound, not just for how governments function, but for the health of democracy itself.

Chapter 10

THE FOURTH ESTATE IN RETREAT

Introduction

In a functioning democracy, the media serves a critical role: interrogating power, informing the citizenry and ensuring accountability. This is the promise of the fourth estate: a counterbalance to the executive, legislative, and judicial branches of government. But that promise has faltered. Today, the Australian media landscape, like its counterparts across liberal democracies, is marked not by fearless scrutiny but by timidity and retreat. The fourth estate has not been abolished, but it has been hollowed out.

The decline has occurred gradually, almost imperceptibly at first, masked by the illusion of abundance. In the digital age, there is no shortage of content: commentary, analysis, opinion and breaking news are available at all hours, across platforms. But volume is no substitute for rigour. Much of what passes for news today is reactive rather than investigative. And as the media's business model has crumbled under the weight of digital disruption and shrinking advertising revenue, the space for serious journalism has narrowed. Outlets chase clicks, reporters are stretched thin, and public interest journalism — the kind that takes time, costs money and risks upsetting those in power — becomes harder to justify.

The rise of ideological echo chambers has further fragmented the media's civic function. Audiences now curate their news consumption to suit their worldview, encouraged by platforms that reward outrage and polarisation. Rather than holding the political class to account, segments of the media have become active participants in the performance, echoing talking points, elevating spectacle over substance and personalising politics to the point of absurdity. In this context, journalism is too often co-opted into the very power structures it was meant to scrutinise. Those "doing political journalism" are largely what you might call unqualified for the discipline.

At the heart of this retreat is a broader institutional decay: a loss of purpose and conviction that mirrors the same hollowing out afflicting politics and the public service. The media is not immune. It has been caught in the same currents. But the consequences of its decline reverberate widely. A media that no longer challenges power enables its further entrenchment. A public that is misinformed or disengaged is easier to manipulate. And a political class unchecked by scrutiny becomes bolder in its evasions, more cynical in its tactics and increasingly comfortable operating in the shadows.

This chapter traces the retreat of the fourth estate through five stages: the erosion of its watchdog function; the rise of ideological silos; the dominance of infotainment; the collapse of sustainable business models; and the complicity of the press in the performative nature of modern politics.

From Watchdog to Lapdog

Once imagined as democracy's fierce defender, the Australian media has, in many quarters, surrendered its watchdog function. Rather than barking at power, too often it sits obediently beside it. The notion that the press should act as an independent check on government, interrogating decisions, exposing corruption and holding public figures to account, now seems more aspirational than operational. In practice, much of contemporary journalism has become either passive, performative or partisan, each a departure from its foundational purpose.

There are structural reasons for this decline. Newsrooms are leaner than they have ever been. Investigative reporting, the kind that once defined journalistic bravery and civic importance, has been gutted by budget constraints and shifting priorities. Fewer journalists are tasked with covering more ground, and beat reporting has been replaced by desk-based aggregation. Under such conditions scrutiny gives way to stenography. Press releases are reported less critically, ministerial announcements become headlines and spin is published with minimal context and inadequate questioning. The cycle of news production has accelerated, and the incentive is no longer to dig deeper but to push content out faster.

Access journalism has compounded the problem. In pursuit of proximity to power, reporters and commentators often temper their critique to maintain relationships with key players. I've made this mistake myself, namely when required to access politicians for television content. The result is a kind of quiet collusion: journalists granted exclusives in return for favourable coverage, or at the very least, a softer touch. It's a dynamic that encourages caution over courage and incentivises complicity. The once-adversarial relationship between press and politics has blurred, and the media's independence suffers accordingly. This is particularly evident during election campaigns, where political leaders control access and punish critical outlets with exclusion. The implicit threat is clear: play the game or you'll be left out of it. Over the years I have been on the plus and minus side of this dance.

The increasing entwinement of journalists and political operatives only deepens the malaise. The revolving door between newsrooms and ministerial offices has long been a feature of Australian public life, but in recent years it has become more overt and more concerning. Journalists become media advisers, advisers return as commentators and the line between reporting and messaging collapses. Familiar faces oscillate between these roles with ease, bringing insider insight but also eroding the boundary that once separated the observer from the participant. When those charged with scrutinising the system are themselves embedded in its machinery, the public interest becomes secondary to insider dynamics and factional loyalties.

These relationships often manifest in commentary that carries the veneer of independence while operating as de facto advocacy. Media figures develop close ties with particular political actors or parties, and their coverage reflects those affiliations. Sometimes it's ideological alignment; other times, it's a matter of access or personal loyalty. Either way, the result is the same: distorted coverage masquerading as objective analysis. The effect is most visible in opinion-heavy programming, particularly on radio and television, where the boundary between journalism and cheerleading is routinely crossed without consequence.

Partisan media outlets further accelerate the retreat. Rather than standing apart from political movements, some publications have willingly become mouthpieces, attacking ideological opponents while shielding allies from criticism. The pretence of neutrality is abandoned, and journalism becomes just another weapon in the culture war. The risk is not merely bias, but the erosion of credibility across the board. When news is indistinguishable from propaganda, trust in the media declines, and with it, trust in democracy. Surveys have consistently shown that public confidence in the media is falling, a trend driven not only by digital disruption but also by perceptions of bias, sensationalism and unreliability.

Public broadcasters, once the bulwark against these trends, have not been immune. Under financial pressure and political attack, even institutions like the ABC have found themselves retreating from fearless scrutiny. The cuts to investigative programs like Four Corners and the winding back of foreign bureaus reflect a broader contraction in scope and ambition. Meanwhile there is too much commentary on the ABC which acts as a giveaway revealing its left wing bias.

Sections of the commercial sector, meanwhile, have embraced a model of journalism that prioritises spectacle over substance. Provocation, conflict, and scandal dominate the headlines, while complex policy debates receive less airtime. Political reporting becomes a theatre of personalities rather than a site of policy interrogation. Journalists chase viral moments, not nuanced understanding. The result is a public discourse that is noisy but shallow, frenetic but easily forgettable. You can hardly blame a sector struggling to remain profitable for playing to its audiences wants which become its strengths.

The rise of the 24-hour news cycle alongside the unending rise of social media dependence has only sharpened these tendencies. Political spin is designed for media environments that demand constant content. The rapid churn of daily headlines rewards tactics over strategy and elevates performative outrage above policy substance. In such an environment, the media becomes less a check on power and more a conduit for its messaging.

This transformation has been gradual, but the consequences are cumulative. Without a robust fourth estate, democratic accountability suffers. Political leaders are emboldened to spin, mislead, and even lie. Confident that the media either won't challenge them or will do so only superficially, with no sustained follow-through. The democratic ideal of an informed citizenry slips further out of reach.

The shift from watchdog to lapdog is not total: there remain journalists and outlets committed to the public good, exposing wrongdoing and challenging power. Their work still matters, and their impact can still be profound. But the space is shrinking, and their influence is increasingly marginal.

The Echo Chamber Effect

One of the most insidious transformations in modern media is the rise of echo chambers: curated spaces where individuals are exposed only to views that reinforce their own. The fragmentation of the media landscape, accelerated by digital technology and social media, has produced a climate in which confirmation bias is the norm. In this environment, the traditional role of the media as a shared space for deliberation and fact-based discourse is diminished. Instead, ideological enclaves form, polarisation deepens and consensus becomes increasingly elusive.

This is not unique to Australia, but the consequences here are profound. Once, Australians largely consumed news from a small number of widely trusted sources. That shared media diet gave the press the power to set the agenda and mediate public discourse. Today, that influence is scattered across an array of digital platforms, each with its own partisan leaning, algorithmic bias and cultural tone. Audiences self-select into news ecosystems that reflect their values, often avoiding opposing views altogether.

Social media platforms have been central to this shift. Designed to maximise engagement, they reward outrage, affirmation and simplicity. Their algorithms elevate content that provokes emotion and encourages tribal loyalty. In such spaces, political nuance is punished and misinformation thrives. Public debate becomes a series of disconnected monologues, each reinforcing its own version of reality.

Traditional media outlets, desperate to remain relevant and financially viable, have often adapted to this fragmented ecosystem by narrowing their editorial focus. Publications chase niche audiences, adopt more overtly partisan positions, and tailor their content to reinforce existing reader prejudices. The result is a form of commercialised echo chamber, where alignment becomes a strategy for survival. Even outlets that claim objectivity are shaped by the pressures of audience retention and digital competition. Balanced reporting rarely trends; ideological fervour does.

Talkback radio and tabloid television have long exploited this dynamic. But now even broadsheets and public broadcasters feel the pull. To remain relevant in an age of attention scarcity, editorial decisions are increasingly made with audience analytics in mind. Editors commission content not just for its public interest value, but for its viral potential. That shift, towards reactive journalism over reflective journalism, feeds the echo chamber effect and accelerates the decline of deliberative democracy.

There is also an institutional cost. Political parties, interest groups and governments no longer see the need to engage across the media spectrum. They target sympathetic outlets, speak directly to loyal constituencies and for the most part ignore critical voices. The traditional press conference, once a forum for scrutiny and accountability, is being increasingly replaced by exclusive drops to favoured journalists or controlled media events. Politicians now often bypass mainstream media altogether, using social platforms to disseminate unfiltered messages to curated audiences. The feedback loop is self-sustaining: politicians play to their base, media outlets play to theirs, and neither engages seriously with disagreement or dissent.

In such an ecosystem, truth becomes contested terrain. There is little agreement on what constitutes a fact, let alone what should be done about it. Expertise is sidelined, conspiracy theories flourish, and public debate becomes unmoored from reality. The media, far from being a corrective, is often an enabler of this trend. By indulging false equivalence — presenting all views as equally valid regardless of evidence — journalists contribute to the confusion rather than cut through it.

The echo chamber effect corrodes more than just public discourse. It undermines social cohesion, breeds cynicism and fosters a politics of grievance. When people live in radically different media realities, the possibility of compromise or shared understanding withers. The fourth estate, which once provided the common language of civic life, is now fragmented and filtered through partisan lenses.

If the media once helped knit a society together through shared facts and national conversation, it now often contributes to pulling it apart. The retreat of the fourth estate isn't only a matter of diminished scrutiny, it's also about diminished connectivity. Without a trusted media landscape in which disagreement can occur productively, democracy is reduced to tribalism, and public engagement becomes a contest of narratives rather than a deliberation over policy and principle.

News as Infotainment

The evolution of news into entertainment has been one of the defining shifts in modern journalism. The line between factual reporting and theatrical performance has blurred to the point of irrelevance in many corners of the media landscape. What once aimed to inform is now often designed to entertain, provoke, or distract. The shift is not just stylistic, it has reshaped the way citizens engage with politics, arguably eroding the quality of public understanding.

This blurring of boundaries has occurred across mediums. Television current affairs programs increasingly resemble reality shows, complete with dramatic music, stylised graphics, and combative formats that privilege personality over substance. The spectacle is the story. Hosts are selected as much for their entertainment value as for journalistic credibility. Political issues are reduced to soundbites, and complex debates are squeezed into confrontational segments designed to produce viral moments rather than considered insights. Investigative news has gone down the same path to some extent.

The commercial incentives are obvious. Outrage generates clicks, conflict draws ratings, and sensationalism sells. In the digital era, attention is the currency of success. Media outlets no longer compete solely on the basis of trustworthiness or rigour, but on their ability to generate traffic, engagement, and shareability. Political journalism has adapted accordingly: dramatising disputes, framing coverage around winners and losers, and foregrounding personalities over policies. It's easier to cover the theatre of leadership tensions or internal party dramas than it is to unpack the nuances of tax reform or healthcare policy, for example.

This form of infotainment has been exacerbated by the rise of commentary-driven formats. Analysis and opinion, once confined to editorial pages, now dominate entire programming blocks across television, radio and online. The pundit class is often made up not of subject-matter experts, but of professional commentators whose primary skill is provocation. Debates are framed as binary contests, and complexity is sacrificed for the sake of clarity, or more accurately for the appearance of clarity.

The danger of this trend is not merely that it trivialises politics, but that it distorts the public's understanding. When journalism prioritises entertainment, the issues that matter most are often underreported or sensationalised. Audiences come away with a skewed picture of what is happening and why. Political leaders, in turn, respond to this shift by performing for the media rather than governing through good policy making. Media management becomes the core skill of successful politicians, and message discipline trumps substantive leadership.

Nowhere is this clearer than in the way leadership coverage is handled. Political leaders are portrayed less as officeholders and more as characters in a long-running drama. Journalists report on their performance, their personal style and their rhetorical flourishes with the same lens applied to celebrities or sports figures. Popularity becomes the central metric, measured obsessively through polls and focus groups. The leader is framed as protagonist or villain, depending on the prevailing narrative. The stakes are rarely policy-based. As a result, leadership contests are treated as cliffhangers rather than as contests of ideas. This approach infects even the public broadcaster.

Social media has turbocharged the entertainment churn. Clips are cut for maximum emotional impact, headlines are optimised for clicks and stories are shaped for shareability rather than substance. In this environment, the news competes not just with other news outlets, but with everything else on the internet: celebrity gossip, memes, influencers, cat videos, you name it. To break through, journalism adopts the same tools: shock, humour and drama. The goal is no longer necessarily to report what matters most, but what will travel fastest.

This logic extends to political coverage. Politicians are aware that they are performing in a media environment shaped by attention economics. They cultivate their own brand, play to the cameras, and engage in staged conflict to draw media attention. Parliamentary exchanges are crafted less for the chamber and more for the evening news or the next morning's front pages. The theatre of politics feeds the theatre of journalism, and both reinforce one another in a cycle of spectacle.

The consequences for democratic engagement are serious. When news is packaged as entertainment, citizens are encouraged to be passive spectators rather than active participants. Political literacy declines, cynicism rises and public trust in institutions erodes. Viewers learn to treat politics as a joke or a soap opera, not as a civic responsibility. The fourth estate, rather than fostering deliberation and accountability, becomes complicit in the performative culture it ought to critique.

The Business Model is Broken

The modern media industry is in a state of economic freefall. The traditional business model that underpinned journalism for much of the twentieth century, anchored in advertising revenue, cross-subsidised departments and stable audience loyalty, has been comprehensively dismantled. In its place is a fragmented digital ecosystem defined by precarious income streams, shrinking newsrooms and a desperate scramble for audience attention. These structural changes have not just altered how journalism is produced and consumed, they have fundamentally weakened the fourth estate's ability to serve as a check on power.

At the core of the crisis is the collapse of advertising as journalism's financial engine. For decades, advertising revenue (both classifieds and display ads) provided the financial foundation for most media outlets. It paid not just for the commercial operations but also, crucially, for the public interest journalism that rarely turned a direct profit. As advertising migrated online, first to digital platforms and then increasingly to the dominant players like Google and Facebook, media companies were left with shrinking slices of a pie that had once been theirs entirely. Classifieds disappeared, the "rivers of gold" dried up as ads moved to the internet. Display ads became cheaper and less lucrative too. And digital advertising, instead of rescuing newsrooms, served only to deepen the crisis, as tech giants absorbed the majority of the revenue while producing none of the content.

The consequences have been dramatic. Traditional newsrooms across Australia have hollowed out. Entire regional newspapers have folded, leaving communities without local reporting and stripping the democratic process of its grassroots scrutiny. In the metropolitan press, foreign bureaus have closed, specialist rounds have been reduced and experienced journalists have been made redundant or forced into generalist roles with heavier workloads and tighter deadlines. Investigative units — costly, time-consuming and resource-intensive — have been scaled back or disbanded altogether. The result is a thinner, shallower press corps, ill-equipped to cover politics with the depth and rigour that democracy demands.

The digital pivot, far from providing a sustainable alternative, has often made things worse. The shift to online platforms forced media organisations to chase clicks as a substitute for subscriptions or display advertising. Audience metrics became central to editorial strategies. Stories are now selected, framed and headlined based on their potential to generate engagement rather than their civic importance. This gave rise to so-called clickbait, sensationalism and a feedback loop which prioritises infotainment.

The impact on political journalism has been particularly acute. Political coverage, once seen as a core public service, is now subject to the same commercial logic as lifestyle content or celebrity gossip. To some extent anyway. Journalists are under pressure to generate content that will 'move' online: opinion pieces, outrage-driven coverage, personality profiles or conflict narratives. Resource-intensive reporting on policy detail, bureaucratic reform, or long-term challenges becomes harder to justify. The economic logic simply doesn't support it. And even when such stories are pursued, they are often buried under a deluge of lighter, faster-moving content.

The emergence of philanthropic models and public-interest

journalism start-ups, such as *The Guardian's* Australian edition or smaller platforms like *The Conversation* and *Crikey* remain marginal in reach, dependent on niche audiences and vulnerable to the same broader market pressures as the bigger players. They also tend to be ideologically biased.

Attempts to address the crisis in the media through government intervention have been patchy and politically fraught. The *News Media Bargaining Code*, legislated in 2021, forced tech giants to pay for Australian news content, but the resulting deals lacked transparency and primarily benefited large established players, most notably News Corp. Smaller outlets were left negotiating from a position of weakness. The underlying asymmetry remains: tech platforms command the audience and the revenue, while traditional media does the journalistic labour without the economic leverage. The hollowing out continues, albeit at a slightly slower pace.

What is left is a media landscape where journalism survives, but on shaky ground. The fundamental tension between profit and public interest has always been present in media markets, but today the balance is dangerously skewed. In the absence of a viable, sustainable financial model, journalism's democratic function — scrutinising power, informing citizens and fostering accountability — is at risk of becoming an afterthought. Political leaders, recognising this, become more adept at media management and spin, knowing the depth of journalistic engagement is limited.

Ultimately, the collapse of the business model is not just a media story, it's a democratic problem. A functioning democracy requires a strong, independent press. When journalism becomes a luxury product, or when its survival depends on the goodwill of billionaires, tech platforms or government largesse, the foundational role of the fourth estate is at risk.

Complicity in the Face of Performative Spin

In an ideal democracy the relationship between politicians and the press is one of mutual tension. The media probes and holds to account, political actors seek to persuade but expect scrutiny. Yet in the hollowed-out landscape of contemporary Australian politics, this balance is no more. Increasingly, the media is complicit in a system of spin, one where narratives are manufactured, dissent is muted and access is traded for compliance.

At the heart of the problem is the rise of access journalism. The logic is simple: reporters rely on political insiders for exclusives, background briefings and scoops. In return, they are expected to play the game, to frame stories in a favourable light. To avoid certain lines of questioning, and, most importantly, not to jeopardise the relationship. It is a form of soft censorship, enforced not through law or regulation, but through the threat of silence. Ask the wrong question, publish an unflattering piece, and the flow of information dries up. I've experienced it when refusing to play the game. In a competitive media market desperate for content, few can afford to be frozen out.

This phenomenon is not unique to Australia, but it is particularly pronounced here given the small size of the national press gallery and the centralisation of political reporting in Canberra. Many journalists covering federal politics have long-standing relationships with the same set of sources (ministers, advisers and spin doctors) who rotate through roles but remain within the same inner circle. This closeness can lead to familiarity, even collegiality, which blunts critical instincts. Reporters become part of the system they are meant to expose. The Australian parliamentary gallery operates out of the parliamentary building, adding proximity to the closeness of relationships. In such an environment spin flourishes, not because it is undetectable, but because calling it out would mean forfeiting access.

The professionalisation of political communication has accentuated the problem. Ministerial offices now include media units staffed by seasoned operatives whose sole function is to manage narratives and control messaging. Entire departments are tasked with framing policy announcements, shaping public opinion and minimising negative coverage. Journalists receive carefully curated information, embargoed and embargo-breaking, accompanied by subtle reminders of what cooperation looks like. In this environment, news becomes not a discovery but a delivery mechanism.

Nowhere is this dynamic more evident than in election coverage. Campaign periods, which should be the apex of political scrutiny, instead become tightly managed performances. Politicians are shielded from unscripted encounters. Media events are choreographed. Questions are limited, often pre-approved, and delivered in controlled settings. Journalists who push too hard are marginalised or excluded altogether. The major parties exploit this environment by reducing policy to slogans and offering little in the way of detail. Coverage, in turn, becomes a theatre of appearances: who looked more "prime ministerial," who won the soundbite war, who made a gaffe. Substance is subsumed by style.

This has real consequences. When media outlets fail to challenge spin, they contribute to the erosion of public trust. Voters are not fooled. They sense the scripted nature of coverage, the absence of genuine engagement, and the repetition of meaningless slogans. They grow cynical, disengaged, or worse susceptible to misinformation and conspiracy. When the media appears complicit in a system that prioritises message control over truth, it creates a vacuum that bad actors are only too willing to fill.

It also distorts political incentives. Politicians learn that spin works, that controlling the narrative, evading hard questions and manipulating media cycles can deliver electoral dividends. The few who attempt to break from the script are punished, either by negative coverage or by the brutal arithmetic of party discipline. Authenticity becomes a liability, further reinforcing the hollow nature of contemporary governance. Media complicity is not the cause, but it can be an enabler.

There are moments of pushback, of course. Journalists have at times refused to play along, fact-checking claims in real time or turning the spotlight on the media-political nexus itself like I am now. But these remain exceptions rather than the rule. They require institutional support, editorial courage and a willingness to sacrifice access in favour of accountability. In an era where media organisations are financially vulnerable and politically cautious, such qualities are increasingly rare.

In a fully functioning democracy, journalists should be adversaries to power, not its echo. The current trajectory suggests the opposite. As spin becomes more sophisticated and the press less resourced and less assertive, the danger is not just bad journalism, it is the normalisation of untruths, the triumph of performance over policy and the slow death of an informed citizenship. Reclaiming the fourth estate's critical role will require more than nostalgia for a lost golden age. It demands structural change, cultural renewal and above all, a recommitment to the foundational belief that truth still matters.

The decline of Australia's media as a robust fourth estate has not occurred in isolation. It reflects and reinforces the broader decay of democratic institutions explored throughout this book. Once a counterweight to political power, the media has been gradually enmeshed within the very system it was meant to scrutinise. The media has become a mirror rather than a check, reflecting back the superficiality, spin, and self-interest of the political class.

Chapter 11
DEMOCRACY IN DECLINE?

The Illusion of Function

Australia remains, on the surface, a functioning democracy. Elections are held regularly, the rule of law is maintained, and the machinery of representative government grinds on in familiar patterns. The decline of democracy is not always loud. It often arrives quietly, through incremental shifts in norms, structures and expectations. A democracy that functions only in name is vulnerable, not just to authoritarian impulses, but to collapse from within.

This chapter examines how Australia's democracy has slipped into what you might call managed decline, sustained by historical institutional momentum but hollowed out. It picks up where the previous chapter left off by assessing the structures of representation, the incentives and disincentives driving political behaviour, and the gradual decoupling of government from those who are governed.

Electoral Disengagement

Australia has long prided itself on being one of the few democracies with compulsory voting, a system designed not only to ensure participation but to bolster legitimacy through near-universal turnout. On the surface, this framework appears to work: election day still sees millions of Australians cast their ballots, with formal turnout typically above 90 per cent. But beneath this statistical veneer lies a more troubling reality. The presence of compulsion masks the depth of disengagement. Citizens may be voting, but they are not participating in any meaningful democratic sense. The act is increasingly mechanical, performed without enthusiasm, conviction or even a basic sense of connection to those seeking office. It is democracy by obligation.

What's become apparent in recent decades is that compulsory voting no longer functions as a proxy for democratic health. Apathy is rising and a growing number of voters deliberately cast informal ballots, spoiling them as an act of protest or indifference. In some electorates, informal votes now exceed ten per cent, and the trend is upward. Even among those who do vote formally, there is a growing pattern of last-minute decisions, minor-party volatility and strategic preference swaps, none of which speak to ideological conviction or policy engagement. The electorate is drifting, not aligning; reacting, not believing.

This disengagement is compounded by the increasingly transactional nature of election campaigns. Voters are no longer treated as active participants in a deliberative process but as segments to be targeted and swayed. Political parties craft messages tailored to narrow demographics (swing voters in marginal seats) while ignoring the broader citizenry. Elections are run through focus groups, polling, and market testing as we've discussed. The language is stripped of substance, loaded with slogans, and delivered with the cadence of advertising. In such a context, it is no wonder voters feel like spectators to a contest that does not speak to them. When politics is reduced to branding, democratic engagement becomes an exercise in brand aversion.

The two-party dominance of Australian politics has also played a central role in this erosion. With Labor and the Coalition oscillating in government and increasingly indistinct in ideology, many voters struggle to see meaningful alternatives. Major parties are perceived as careerist machines, driven more by power than principle. Minor parties, while often reflecting real discontent, frequently lack the capacity or coherence to offer constructive solutions. The rise of independents and micro-parties in recent elections has reflected not so much a resurgence of democratic vitality as a fragmented protest: a symptom of systemic disaffection. Voters are grasping for alternatives not because they are inspired, but because they are exhausted by what's on offer.

There is also a growing demographic divide in political engagement. Young Australians are particularly alienated from formal politics. Enrolment rates among first-time voters lag, trust in politicians is at historic lows and traditional forms of civic participation such as joining parties, campaigning and engaging with policy are now the preserve of a narrow and ageing elite. Young people still care about political issues, but they increasingly express this through activism, online discourse or disengagement, rather than through the ballot box. Democracy, as institutionalised in Australia, feels remote and unresponsive.

This alienation is not just emotional, it is structural. The centralisation of power within political parties, the executive dominance of the Prime Minister's office, and the rigid control over messaging and policy leave little room for genuine responsiveness. Voters can change governments, but they cannot meaningfully shape policy debates between elections. Public consultations are often tokenistic, citizen juries are rare and parliamentary committees are either ignored or used for theatre. For many Australians the idea that voting changes anything substantial is increasingly implausible.

Technology has added to this dynamic, creating both opportunity and risk. On the one hand, digital platforms have enabled new forms of engagement, but these tools often sit outside the formal political system. On the other, they have fuelled disinformation, polarisation, and echo chambers. Political discourse online is often dominated by outrage, misinformation and superficiality. Citizens are more connected, but not necessarily more informed or empowered. Worse still, the political class has learned to exploit these channels simply to manipulate sentiment, using algorithms and micro-targeting to divide and distract.

Compulsory voting may still compel attendance, but it cannot manufacture meaning. The ritual of voting is not enough to sustain democracy if the content of democratic life is drained of purpose. The formalities of electoral democracy remain intact, but the public's belief in the efficacy of those processes has been profoundly shaken. To be sure, the malaise isn't a reason to shift from compulsory voting, that would be a case of throwing the baby out with the bath water. Compulsory voting is globally unique but it ensures that sections of society aren't left behind in the democratic process purely because they are disenfranchised enough to choose not to vote. But we absolutely need to fix our democratic polity at its core to take advantage of the inclusiveness compulsory voting can support.

When citizens participate in elections without believing in their significance, the democratic system risks losing its legitimacy. It becomes a hollow process, vulnerable to populism, cynicism and manipulation. Voters become more susceptible to simplistic solutions and charismatic outsiders promising to "drain the swamp" or disrupt the status quo. Electoral disengagement thus becomes a breeding ground for democratic decay: not because people stop voting, but because they stop believing that voting matters.

This chapter does not suggest that electoral democracy in Australia has failed entirely. But it does argue that its foundations are weaker than they appear. The legitimacy once derived from high turnout is no longer sufficient. What is needed is a reconnection between citizens and the state. Restoring democratic faith will not be achieved by marketing campaigns or tweaks to voting procedures. It will require a deeper reform of political culture, one that places the citizen, not the strategist, back at the centre of democratic life.

Parliamentary Theatre

If elections have become hollow rituals of democracy, then Parliament — once the grand stage of deliberation and accountability — has become its most theatrical set-piece. The Australian Parliament still convenes, laws are debated and Question Time is televised. But increasingly, these proceedings represent performance over purpose. The chamber designed to host meaningful debate and represent a plurality of voices now too often stages political theatre, with outcomes predetermined by party discipline and dialogue reduced to soundbites aimed at the evening news cycle.

This erosion of parliamentary function is institutional. Power has steadily drifted away from the floor of Parliament and into the hands of the executive. Ministers, backed by party machines, dominate the legislative agenda. Backbenchers (particularly those from the major parties) are largely spectators to their own government's business. Their capacity to dissent is curtailed not only by convention but by preselection threats and career considerations. In this environment, independence of thought is discouraged, and parliamentary debate becomes a symbolic formality.

Question Time, in theory, should serve as a moment of rigorous scrutiny. An opportunity for the opposition to test the government's competence, integrity and policy agenda. In practice, it has become a showcase of partisan pantomime. Questions are framed not to elicit information but to score political points. Answers are evasive, rehearsed, and dripping with spin. The Speaker is often drawn from the ruling party and seldom exercises impartial discipline, although there have been improvements on this narrow front in recent years. Viewers watching from the public gallery or on television see a cacophony of shouting, smirking and staged indignation.

Committees, once regarded as the deliberative engine rooms of the Parliament, have also been diminished. Their role in scrutinising legislation, investigating public policy issues and holding the executive to account has been undermined by partisanship and executive interference. Government majorities on key committees ensure that critical findings are neutered, inquiries are steered away from sensitive topics and uncomfortable truths can be buried. When committees do produce robust reports, they are often ignored. And too many committees lack the know-how to properly investigate problematic areas of our system, instead using their platforms to generate headlines without substance or understanding of the issues.

One of the more subtle contributors to parliamentary theatre is the increasing centralisation of political messaging. The rise of the "media adviser" class and the dominance of leader-focused communications strategies have meant that MPs are often prohibited from expressing personal views, engaging in policy innovation or responding authentically to constituent concerns. Every utterance is subject to message discipline. Every appearance is filtered through party talking points. The result is a homogeneity of expression that flattens debate and reduces parliamentary proceedings to a contest of branding.

The decline in parliamentary standards has not gone unnoticed by the public either. Surveys consistently show that trust in Parliament as an institution is falling. Citizens perceive it as insular, combative and out of touch. Simply put, it's a hostile workplace. This is not simply a matter of poor optics, it reflects the reality of a chamber that no longer functions as a true forum for national deliberation.

As Parliament becomes more theatrical, media coverage focuses on the drama. Journalists report on who "won" Question Time rather than what was said. I used to host a post Question Time show that did exactly that. Social media amplifies the most inflammatory clips, rewarding performative outrage over reasoned argument. Politicians, aware of the incentives, lean further into the spectacle. Those who resist the theatrics are either drowned out or dismissed as naïve.

To be clear, political performance has always been a part of parliamentary life. Rhetoric, showmanship and partisanship are nothing new. But the balance has tipped. The performative elements have overwhelmed the deliberative ones. What has changed is not the presence of theatre, but the absence of consequence. Debates do not influence outcomes, questions do not prompt answers, and accountability is rarely secured. The entire process has become a set piece.

Moreover, the decline of meaningful deliberation has broader implications for policy quality. When legislation is drafted behind closed doors, rushed through under guillotine motions, or passed without adequate scrutiny, the result is poorer governance. Complex issues are oversimplified, unintended consequences are missed, and policy becomes reactive rather than considered. Parliament should be the place where competing ideas are tested, refined, and legitimised. Instead, it too often acts as a rubber stamp for executive will, with all the ceremony and none of the substance.

Institutional Decay

A functioning democracy relies on more than just elections and parliaments. It depends on a constellation of institutions: electoral commissions, watchdogs, integrity bodies, courts, and statutory agencies. These provide the scaffolding for democratic governance and are the instruments through which power is checked, transparency enforced and rights protected. But in Australia, as in many liberal democracies, these institutions have not been immune to erosion. Their capacity to operate independently, and their authority to hold power to account, have been gradually diminished. Institutional decay has set in.

This decay is most evident in the weakening of accountability bodies. Institutions like the Australian National Audit Office (ANAO), the Commonwealth Ombudsman, and now the National Anti-Corruption Commission (NACC) were designed to ensure government integrity. But their effectiveness depends on political will, adequate resourcing and cultural respect for their independence. Too often, they are starved of funding, marginalised in their remit, or attacked when their findings are politically inconvenient. The ANAO's reports, for instance, have repeatedly highlighted waste, mismanagement, and pork-barrelling, only to be dismissed or ignored by those in power. Rather than prompting reform the exposure of failure is met with defensiveness almost every time.

Electoral institutions are not immune either. While the Australian Electoral Commission (AEC) remains one of the more robust components of our democratic infrastructure, it too has faced resource constraints and political pressure. Debates around electoral redistribution, party registration and campaign financing have become increasingly fraught, with major parties often pursuing reforms designed to entrench their own advantage rather than strengthen the system as a whole. Loopholes in donation disclosure remain wide open. 'Dark money' continues to flow into party coffers, often undisclosed until well after elections have passed, if at all.

Perhaps most disturbingly, the very idea of an independent public institution has come under sustained rhetorical attack. When media organisations, judges or statutory bodies issue findings unfavourable to the government of the day, they are increasingly branded as partisan or out of touch. This denigration erodes the legitimacy of institutions and shifts the public debate away from facts and accountability towards narrative and spin. It reflects a political culture more interested in control than good governance.

This process of institutional decay is slow-burning but deeply consequential. Unlike a constitutional crisis, which sparks immediate public concern, this form of erosion is gradual and often invisible to the casual observer. But its effects are profound. When watchdogs lose their teeth, when public servants fear speaking truth to power, when transparency is procedural rather than real, democracy is no longer safeguarded.

Australia is not unique in this regard. Across the democratic world, we see similar patterns of decline: the politicisation of institutions, the hollowing out of accountability, the corrosion of trust. What makes Australia's case distinct is the complacency with which this decay is met. There is little public outcry, few political consequences and even less reform. The slow dismantling of our institutional architecture continues not because the public approves, but because attention is elsewhere, drawn to the latest headline, scandal or leadership spill.

This institutional fragility becomes particularly dangerous in times of crisis. Whether dealing with a pandemic, economic downturn or environmental disaster, democracies rely on strong leaders, as discussed earlier, and equally strong, credible institutions to coordinate responses and maintain public trust. A weakened public service, politicised health bodies and questioned integrity agencies all impair crisis management. When institutions are perceived as partisan or incompetent, compliance falters and social cohesion frays.

Democracy as a Brand

Democracy, once understood as a robust system of representation, accountability, and citizen engagement, has increasingly become a branding exercise. Politicians invoke the term with reverence. Yet beneath this democratic branding lies a more cynical reality: many of the structural and procedural features that define a healthy democracy have withered. What remains is a democratic aesthetic masking a hollow core.

Once again, Australia is not alone in this. Across liberal democracies, leaders continue to declare their fidelity to democratic values while simultaneously undermining the very institutions and norms that sustain them. But in the Australian context, the branding of democracy is particularly stark. Electoral rituals are maintained. Parliaments sit. Statutory agencies exist. Yet their functioning is increasingly ceremonial. Voters are encouraged to believe they are participants in a vibrant political system, but their choices are constrained, their voices diluted, and their influence limited.

This performative form of democracy is marked by superficial gestures. Governments consult the public, but often after decisions have been made. Parliamentary committees hold inquiries, but their recommendations are ignored and sometimes divorced from reality. Integrity bodies are created with fanfare, only to be underfunded and politically constrained. These mechanisms serve as symbols of democratic legitimacy, but rarely shape outcomes in meaningful ways.

The language of democracy is central to this performance. Political leaders invoke "the will of the people" to justify decisions, even when those decisions contradict public sentiment or bypass deliberative processes. Referendums, when held, are carefully stage-managed or avoided altogether if the outcome is uncertain. Engagement strategies are designed to be seen rather than heard, performed in the media rather than acted upon in policy terms.

Part of the reason this branding is so effective is that democracy itself is widely admired but poorly understood. Many citizens equate democracy solely with elections, overlooking the broader architecture required to support it: a free press, independent institutions, a vibrant civil society and a responsive public service. Elected dictatorships are not true democracies. This narrow understanding enables governments to meet minimal democratic expectations, regular elections and peaceful transfers of power. All the while neglecting the substantive demands of transparency, participation and accountability.

Media plays an enabling role here. Political reporting often uncritically reproduces the symbols of democracy without interrogating their efficacy. Press conferences, parliamentary announcements and budget speeches are broadcast as markers of democratic action, even when they are devoid of real consequence. There is little space in mainstream political journalism for sustained institutional critique. The rituals are covered; the hollowing out is rarely investigated.

When democratic institutions are repeatedly used as props in a political performance, trust is eroded. Citizens lose faith not just in those wielding power, but in the democratic system itself. The branding of democracy, in this sense, becomes self-defeating. By substituting symbolism for substance, it undermines the very legitimacy it seeks to project.

Restoring democracy as a lived experience rather than a label will require effort. It means moving beyond ritual to reform: strengthening institutions, enhancing participation and embedding accountability in everyday governance. It means resisting the temptation to reduce politics to optics, and insisting instead on substance. A healthy democracy cannot be merely marketed; it must be lived, tested, and renewed through constant civic engagement.

The crisis of civic confidence is particularly pronounced among younger Australians. Polling consistently shows that younger cohorts are more sceptical of democratic institutions than older generations.

Many express the view that democracy serves the powerful rather than the people, that voting changes little, and that politics is rigged in favour of entrenched interests. While some of this sentiment is generational disaffection, it also reflects lived experiences of growing inequality, environmental degradation and political inertia. Without meaningful change, this temporary disillusionment may calcify into permanent disengagement.

What makes this crisis particularly dangerous is that it often goes unacknowledged by those in power. Political leaders continue to invoke the language of trust, transparency and public engagement, while presiding over systems that alienate and frustrate voters. Efforts to restore confidence are typically reactive, triggered by scandal or electoral backlash, rather than proactive. A genuine strategy to rebuild civic trust would require a fundamental rethinking of political culture, institutional design, and citizen participation. Yet such reform is rarely prioritised, because those who benefit from the current arrangements have all the power and little incentive to change them.

Chapter 12

'REFORM' WITHOUT COURAGE

Reform is the lifeblood of democratic progress. It is the mechanism through which systems adapt, evolve, and respond to new challenges. In Australia, reform has been the foundation of key national achievements: from universal healthcare and compulsory superannuation to economic liberalisation and gun control. But in recent decades, the willingness to pursue reform has waned. The political appetite for bold, structural change has diminished. Where once leaders staked their reputations on reshaping the nation, today they tiptoe around tough decisions, prioritising political survival over policy substance. I'm not even sure many of them understand its importance anymore.

This retreat from reform is not merely a matter of poor leadership, it reflects a deeper malaise within the Australian polity. The rewards for policy ambition have declined, while the risks have grown. Short-term media cycles, opposition tactics, and a hyper-fragmented electorate punish complexity and nuance. Political leaders have learned to manage perception rather than confront entrenched problems. In this climate, courage becomes a liability and consensus is a rarity. The result is inertia masquerading as prudence.

It is not that reform is no longer needed, on the contrary the case for renewal is overwhelming. Whether it's housing affordability, tax simplification, federation reform or energy resilience, the evidence is clear and the need is urgent. Yet time and again, proposals are shelved, white papers gather dust, and consultations lead nowhere. Australia now operates within a culture of deferred reform: a political landscape where acknowledgement of a problem rarely leads to its resolution.

This chapter investigates the architecture of this failure. It examines how the major parties have become risk-averse, why public servants shy away from ambitious policy design, and how media scrutiny can both illuminate and intimidate reform efforts. It also considers the structural inhibitors that have turned reform from a leadership imperative into a political gamble: parliamentary gridlock, intergovernmental rivalry, and the influence of vested interests. Together, these dynamics have created a system allergic to change, even as the case for change only grows stronger.

From Hawke to Hollowing Out

Australia's political history is punctuated by moments of genuine reformist ambition: periods when governments confronted difficult issues head-on, reshaped policy frameworks, and dared to disrupt the status quo. The reform era of the 1980s and early 1990s, under the Hawke and Keating Labor governments, stands as a benchmark. It was a time when political leaders pursued structural change with clear-eyed purpose, often at significant political risk. Tariff reductions, financial deregulation, enterprise bargaining, superannuation, and tax reform were all landmark achievements. These were not reforms born of convenience or electoral expediency. They were hard-won transformations, often involving compromise, confrontation, and sustained public argument.

What made this era exceptional was not simply the scope of change, but the political culture that enabled it. Reform was viewed as a public good. Political leaders spoke in terms of national interest, not just electoral strategy. There was a willingness to educate the public, to build support through persuasion rather than spin, and to wear the consequences when reforms generated backlash. The ACTU's involvement in the *Prices and Incomes Accord* typified this approach: governments working alongside interest groups. The economic rationalism of the period was contested, and its social impacts debated, but the direction was clear: modernise the economy and prepare Australia for global competition.

The Howard government, which succeeded Keating in 1996, demonstrated flashes of reformist intent. The introduction of the Goods and Services Tax (GST) was a bold and electorally risky move, particularly given Howard's earlier "never ever" promise on the matter. It was taken to an election, won narrowly, and implemented through delicate negotiations with the Australian Democrats in the Senate. The *National Competition Policy*, a legacy of earlier agreements between federal and state governments, was extended and institutionalised under Howard. Again, this required building consensus and enduring sustained opposition.

Yet as the years progressed, the political will to pursue reform steadily waned, other than on the industrial relations front in Howard's final term. The Rudd and Gillard governments faced real opportunities, on carbon pricing, education funding and health system restructuring, but were undermined by internal party instability, relentless media cycles, Senate gridlock and unrelenting negativity from the official Opposition. While some reforms did pass, they were often compromised, poorly explained, or reversed under subsequent governments. The Abbott government's "budget repair" agenda was framed as reformist but lacked the legitimacy and political skill to carry the public with it. Meanwhile, the Turnbull and Morrison governments rarely sought to engage in structural reform at all, preferring rhetorical gestures and minor policy tweaks over wholesale change.

This trajectory, from the boldness of Hawke to the policy caution of recent years, reflects a broader hollowing out of political leadership. The idea that government exists to shape society and drive progress has been eclipsed by a managerial mindset: maintain stability, avoid controversy, win the next election. Reform is no longer pursued as a principled end, but simply through the prism of political risk management. It is only contemplated when it can be sold as low-cost, low-conflict and preferably bipartisan. Conditions that are increasingly hard to meet.

Compounding this shift is the media environment in which reform proposals now live or die. In the 1980s and 1990s, political leaders had more time and space to make their case. Daily news cycles were slower, and long-form journalism provided avenues for serious policy debate. Today's 24/7 media landscape rewards immediacy over substance. Proposals are leaked, attacked, and sometimes abandoned before they are even properly explained. Reformers find themselves on the defensive, forced to fight media-fuelled scare campaigns that distort their intentions and erode public support before a word of legislation is drafted.

The fragmentation of the electorate has also made reform harder. In the Hawke and Keating era, the political centre was broader, and major parties commanded the allegiance of most voters. Today, with minor parties and independents occupying a growing share of the vote, governments must negotiate complex parliamentary dynamics just to survive. Reform that alienates any one group can trigger a swift backlash and political destabilisation. It creates a form of policy paralysis, where the cost of action outweighs the perceived benefits.

There is also the influence of vested interests. Reforms that challenge corporate power or entrench privileges now face heavily resourced opposition campaigns. The mining tax, which played a central role in the demise of both the Rudd and Gillard governments, is a case in point. Designed to capture a fairer share of profits during the boom years, it was demolished through a multi-million-dollar industry campaign and abandoned shortly after. The lesson for politicians was clear: ambition invites attacks. For those more interested in holding office than using it for change, the rational response is to avoid reforms altogether.

All of this has created a deeply risk-averse political culture. Politicians are not rewarded for bravery, but they are punished for overreach. The public, meanwhile, has grown increasingly sceptical that governments can deliver anything meaningful at all. This erosion of trust feeds a vicious cycle: the less politicians attempt reform, the more citizens disengage; the more disengaged the public becomes, the less mandates exist for real change.

In the space of a generation, reform has shifted from being the defining task of government to an aspiration so fraught with danger that it is rarely attempted. The hollow state, in this context, is not just one of declining capacity but one of shrinking ambition. A political class once driven by ideas and outcomes is now motivated by risk mitigation and media strategy. The boldness of a Hawke or a Howard seems not only distant, but almost unimaginable under current conditions. The challenge now is not just to remember what was possible, but to ask why it no longer is.

Policy Paralysis

At the heart of Australia's reform drought lies a condition more debilitating than simple caution: policy paralysis. This is not merely the absence of action, but the entrenchment of inaction. It is the structural inability of governments to progress even widely accepted reforms, trapped in a system that punishes boldness, rewards delay, and makes even minor policy adjustments politically hazardous. While the political class often gestures at change, the machinery of government now operates in a way that neutralises ambition, dilutes vision, and produces policy outcomes only when absolutely unavoidable.

One major cause of this paralysis is the calcification of the public service. Once a site of policy innovation and fearless advice, the bureaucracy has become increasingly cautious, politicised, and management-driven, as we've discussed previously. Departments are incentivised to avoid controversy, to conform to ministerial expectations, and to produce outputs rather than outcomes. Complex, long-term policy thinking has been subordinated to short-term political optics. As I've argued elsewhere, the rise of the managerial class within both politics and the public service has meant that technical competence is now prioritised over intellectual curiosity or ideological clarity. Public servants have become risk managers, not policy designers.

Parliamentary dysfunction is another key ingredient. Successive governments have struggled to control the Senate, making the passage of controversial reforms an exhausting exercise in compromise. Minority governments and hung parliaments have become more common, elevating the influence of crossbenchers whose support must be courted issue by issue. Even when governments enjoy a lower house majority, their capacity to enact reform is frequently stymied by an upper house that acts as a brake on legislative ambition. This fragmentation in the post Australian Democrats years has encouraged governments to avoid difficult issues entirely, relying instead on executive action, budget tinkering, and announcement politics.

The obstructionist nature of contemporary politics reinforces this paralysis. Where once the major parties might compete over how best to deliver necessary reforms, today they more often seek to exploit them for short-term tactical advantage. Bipartisanship has become a rarity on the issues that matter, and when it does appear, it is often used to neutralise an issue rather than to resolve it. Political point-scoring has replaced policy debate. Opposition parties frequently reverse their stance once in government, contributing to a cycle of inconsistency and erosion of trust. The treatment of carbon pricing over the past two decades is a textbook example: a whiplash-inducing sequence of introductions, repeals, rebrands, and rhetorical pivots that has left the policy landscape more confusing than when it began.

The media's role in this dynamic cannot be understated. As explored in Chapter 10, the 24-hour news cycle, combined with the rise of tabloid-style reporting and social media outrage, has made it significantly harder to conduct measured policy debate. Politicians are forced to pre-empt attack lines and media blowback before a policy is even announced. Leaks derail processes, scare campaigns are mounted in real-time, and nuance is sacrificed in favour of slogan-ready talking points. In such an environment, it is safer not to propose reform than to risk being on the defensive from the moment it enters public consciousness. That said, it is the job of the politicians to overcome these challenges.

Policy paralysis is also sustained by the changing expectations of voters. Australians have become more sceptical of major parties and more distrustful of government promises. After decades of reform delivering uneven benefits, there is now widespread suspicion that new policies are thinly veiled cuts or only serve narrow interests. This has led to an electorate that demands action but punishes implementation. Citizens want housing affordability fixed but reject zoning reforms. They want climate action but oppose changes to fuel taxes or energy infrastructure. This contradictory mindset reflects not just voter self-interest but the failure of political leaders to build and maintain public trust.

Taken together, these forces have created a system in which governments feel both compelled to promise reform and incapable of delivering it. Major reviews are commissioned and never acted upon. The rhetoric of reform remains: Prime ministers continue to promise bold agendas, but it is often little more than performative governance. The hollowing out of state capacity has been accompanied by the hollowing out of reform as a serious undertaking.

The Cost of Courage

In an era defined by political risk aversion, the few leaders who have attempted genuine reform have been slapped down. Consider Julia Gillard's carbon pricing scheme. Whatever one's view of its design or efficacy, the reform was substantial and driven by an ambition to tackle climate change through a market-based mechanism. Yet Gillard's political execution, especially her now-infamous declaration that "there will be no carbon tax under a government I lead," left her exposed. The Coalition, led by Tony Abbott, seized on the broken-promise narrative with relentless aggression. Aided by sympathetic sections of the media, the policy was framed as an existential threat to households and businesses alike. Gillard's leadership never recovered, and the carbon pricing mechanism was repealed under Abbott, only to be replaced with a less effective alternative.

Kevin Rudd, too, paid the price for reformist ambition. His initial surge in popularity was tied to his promise to be a "policy wonk" prime minister. He staked his government's credibility on the Carbon Pollution Reduction Scheme, and when the Senate blocked it, Rudd shelved the plan, sparking a crisis of legitimacy. The perception that he had abandoned his core principles, followed by erratic administrative behaviour, allowed party colleagues to justify his removal. Reform was both his calling card and his undoing.

Even John Howard, one of the country's most successful electoral politicians and a reformer to boot, was not immune. His WorkChoices legislation, introduced after he secured control of both houses of parliament in 2007, reflected a bold ideological commitment to industrial relations reform. Yet the absence of a clear public mandate, combined with an aggressive union-led campaign, transformed the policy into an albatross. It dominated the 2007 election campaign and contributed directly to the Coalition's defeat. The lesson for those who followed was stark: even successful leaders can fall when they push too hard.

The political cost of courage is not restricted to prime ministers. State premiers, treasurers, and ministers at all levels have faced similar consequences. Campbell Newman's sweeping public sector cuts in Queensland, Mike Baird's controversial lockout laws in New South Wales, and even Anna Bligh's asset sales in the wake of the global financial crisis each provoked public backlash disproportionate to the reforms themselves. The media's framing, the opposition's opportunism, and the electorate's scepticism converged to punish those willing to confront hard truths, even when the underlying policy rationale was sound. You could argue the same when it came to Bill Shorten's policy manifesto from opposition in 2019.

The modern political environment sends a clear message: bold reformers will not be rewarded. They may be lauded in hindsight, once the consequences of inaction become clear, but in the moment they are politically isolated. The incentives are all skewed. Ministers who play it safe and avoid controversy are more likely to enjoy long tenures. Backbenchers who toe the party line and avoid difficult votes retain preselection. Party leaders who manage the media cycle and neutralise divisive issues are celebrated as savvy strategists, regardless of whether they achieve substantive outcomes. Opposition leaders who embrace a small target win as long as the times suit them.

The result is a feedback loop of mediocrity. Courage becomes the exception. Policy ambition is constrained not by practical limits but by a lack of political imagination. The most successful politicians are often those who promise little, deliver even less, and avoid attracting attention. Reform, when it happens, tends to be either cosmetic or the product of a crisis: triggered not by vision, but by the collapse of the status quo.

This also affects the calibre of those who enter politics. Reform-minded individuals, particularly from policy or academic backgrounds, are increasingly deterred from public life. They see what happens to those who challenge orthodoxy and conclude that meaningful change is better pursued from outside parliament: via advocacy, journalism or civil society. Meanwhile, those who do succeed in politics are often selected more for their media skills, factional loyalty or capacity to avoid missteps than for their ideas or policy acumen.

What emerges is a political culture in which cowardice is incentivised and boldness penalised. This culture cannot be changed overnight, but it can be understood—and understanding is the first step towards changing it.

Rhetoric Without Reform

In an environment where genuine reform is politically perilous, governments have increasingly substituted rhetoric into the equation. The language of ambition endures: Prime ministers still claim to be "nation builders", ministers speak of "once-in-a-generation reforms", and white papers are launched with great fanfare. But behind the proclamations lies a hollowness. Much of what passes for policy development today is performative, designed not to reshape the nation but to signal intent, neutralise criticisms or simply fill the airwaves. Australia has entered an era of announcement politics where the illusion of reform suffices to cover the absence of substantive action.

One clear example is infrastructure policy. Announcements of major projects are often made multiple times once funding is allocated. More coverage follows when planning begins, and again when construction commences. Governments bank the political benefit each time, regardless of how delayed or diminished the actual delivery becomes, or if costs blow out. Projects are rebadged or re-announced under successive administrations. It becomes hard to recall who was actually responsible for its inception. The substantive question of whether the infrastructure is needed, or well integrated into broader planning frameworks, becomes secondary to the political utility of the announcement itself.

The same dynamic is evident in climate policy. Governments across the political divide have adopted net-zero targets and clean energy commitments while quietly continuing fossil fuel subsidies and approving new coal and gas projects. The language of environmental stewardship is used to deflect criticism, even as the underlying policy settings remain largely unchanged. This disjunction between words and actions corrodes public trust and deepens voter cynicism.

Political communication strategies reinforce this shift. Media advisers and spin doctors now play a central role in shaping not only how policy is sold, but whether it is pursued at all. The focus is not on outcomes, but on optics. What matters is how a policy is framed, how it plays in key demographics, and whether it can be leveraged against opponents. This approach rewards superficial messaging over substantive engagement. Instead of explaining the complexities of reform, leaders fall back on slogans, fear campaigns and misdirection.

The rise of social media and the 24-hour news cycle compounds this problem. In such an environment, attention is fleeting and narratives are fragile. Governments are encouraged to make announcements quickly and often, to dominate the media cycle regardless of substance.

This favours constant activity over considered planning. Policy processes are condensed, consultation truncated, and stakeholder engagement reduced to a box-ticking exercise. In the rush to generate headlines, depth is lost and with it, the potential for lasting change.

Rhetoric without reform also serves a more insidious function: it allows governments to posture as ambitious while avoiding accountability for failure. When a reform does not materialise, ministers can blame external factors: the Senate, economic headwinds, or global uncertainty, while pointing to their stated intent as evidence of commitment. The policy failure is thus reframed as a consequence of circumstances. This rhetorical sleight of hand lets politicians claim the mantle of reformer without ever taking the associated risks to make it happen.

This mode of governance is not merely a symptom of political weakness, it is learned failure. Reform becomes a branding exercise, a series of talking points, a placeholder for conviction. Even ambitious policy agendas, like Labor's "Future Made in Australia" plan or Coalition pushes for nuclear energy, are stripped of transformative content and reconstituted as slogans.

The cost of this shift is profound. It breeds a culture of distrust, where citizens struggle to distinguish between genuine intent and political theatre. It hollows out institutions, which are repurposed to support messaging rather than policymaking. It discourages innovation, as departments become more focused on feeding the media machine than developing coherent strategies. And it demoralises public servants and stakeholders who engage in good faith, only to find that their contributions are ultimately ignored.

The Reform Void

If the cost of courage has risen and rhetoric has replaced reform, then what remains is a vacuum: a reform void at the heart of Australian governance. This void is not merely a temporary lull between ambitious agendas. It has become structural, embedded in political culture, institutional arrangements and public expectations. It has become a serious problem.

Once, Australian governments were among the most reformist in the world. The 1980s and early 1990s saw a flurry of activity: financial deregulation, trade liberalisation, the floating of the dollar, the expansion of HECS, superannuation reform, and the Prices and Incomes Accord. Earlier in the life of our Commonwealth we pioneered compulsory voting, giving women the right to vote and represent, and using different methods of counting votes, such as preferencing and proportional representation.

Whether from the left or right, governments understood that their legitimacy derived not merely from holding office, but from shaping the nation. Reform required hard choices, but there was a sense of shared purpose and a willingness to expend political capital and think outside the square. Not anymore.

Today, that instinct has withered. Reform is no longer the organising principle of government. It is an afterthought, deployed only when a crisis makes it unavoidable. The political class has internalised the idea that ambition is risky, and the public has adjusted its expectations accordingly. Voters no longer look to government for vision, they hope only for competence.

This is not simply a failure of individual leadership, it has become systemic. The media punishes complexity and nuance. Parties prioritise message discipline over open debate. Internal democracy is weakened by party internals, limiting the space for new ideas. Public servants, now politicised and cautious, are less inclined to offer bold advice. Think tanks and advocacy groups struggle to break through the noise. Reform is not just avoided; it is pre-emptively neutered by a system that anticipates opposition and moves to minimise conflict before it even arises.

The result is stagnation. Tax reform is placed in the too-hard basket, federation reforms too, despite widespread recognition that the system is unsustainable. Climate change policy remains a patchwork of state initiatives and ad hoc federal measures, and they keep changing. Health and education funding are managed through short-term agreements rather than structural redesign, such that throwing money at the problem seems to be the only idea anyone now has. Intergenerational inequality worsens, with younger Australians locked out of housing and burdened by insecure work, yet little is done by way of state and federal collaboration to redress the imbalance. These are not new problems, they are well known.

In this context, the very idea of reform begins to lose its meaning. Politicians speak of "reform" when making administrative changes, tinkering with settings, or introducing pilot programs. Substantial change (redistributive, structural, forward-looking) has been replaced with managerial adjustment. The void is filled with spin, not substance.

The hollowing out of reformist ambition fuels public cynicism, which in turn discourages further attempts at meaningful change. This vicious cycle entrenches disengagement. Voters no longer believe politicians will improve their lives, and politicians sensing the mistrust retreat further into defensive postures. Participation wanes, civil society weakens and populists exploit the vacuum by offering simple answers to complex problems.

To move beyond the reform void, there must first be an acknowledgement of its existence. Political leaders must recognise that governing without ambition is not neutral, it is a form of failure. Institutions must be recalibrated to reward long-term thinking rather than short-term survival. Citizens must reassert their expectations, demanding more than competence or charisma. And the media must resist the temptation to reduce every policy debate to a personality clash or electoral horse race.

In the next chapter, Power Without Purpose, the focus shifts from the absence of reform to the broader question of what governance is in an era where conviction is absent, policy is performative, and institutions are under strain. If reform has vacated the stage, what remains in its place? And what does it mean to hold power in a system that no longer knows what to do with it?

Chapter 13

POWER WITHOUT PURPOSE

Power in democratic systems is supposed to be a means to an end. It is sought in order to govern, and governance is meant to be directed by purpose: whether ideological, philosophical or simply grounded in a commitment to public service. But in the modern Australian context, this connection has frayed. Increasingly, political power is pursued and wielded not to realise a vision or deliver reform, but for its own sake. It has become the ultimately hollow prize at the end of a tactical game.

This is the logical consequence of the dynamics explored in earlier chapters: the collapse of conviction, the rise of the managerial class, the substitution of spin for substance and the retreat from reform. In such an environment political actors are incentivised to chase office without clear answers to the question of what they will do with it.

The symptoms are everywhere: leaders who arrive in office with no real agenda beyond branding exercises and slogans; cabinets that drift from one media cycle to the next; governments that accumulate political capital but are unwilling to spend it. Without a sense of purpose, power itself becomes unstable, incapable of delivering anything lasting. The very idea of political leadership as a vehicle for change has been diminished.

This chapter explores how power has been unmoored from purpose in contemporary Australian politics. It begins by examining how political office has become an empty prize, sought for reasons that have little to do with policy outcomes. It then considers how leadership itself has been diminished. With governments focused on the next election rather than the next decade, meaningful planning is displaced by short thinking.

If those in power are not guided by conviction, ambition, or reformist zeal, what then is the point of governance? What happens to public trust, civic identity and institutional legitimacy when politics offers no direction? These are the questions at the heart of the hollow state.

The Empty Prize

Political office in Australia has become increasingly transactional. In this context, the attainment of power is less about what it enables and more about what it represents: victory, status, validation. But stripped of larger meaning, power becomes an empty prize. This dynamic is not unique to any one side of politics. Labor and the Coalition have both, in recent years, demonstrated a tendency to treat electoral success as an end in itself.

In the absence of conviction, tactical nous becomes the chief political virtue. Leaders are chosen not for their ideas but for their electoral appeal. The skills that matter are those of message discipline, factional manoeuvring and media management. The political class becomes defined by its ability to win, and increasingly by its inability to do much once it has.

The early days of a new administration, once used to implement bold reforms, are now devoted to settling nerves, projecting stability and avoiding mistakes. The so-called "first hundred days" are often deliberately cautious now, unless we are talking about Donald Trump's second term as President. Ministers are told to be disciplined, to "stay in their lane," and to avoid distraction. Caution becomes the operating mode. Even long-term incumbents, having built considerable political capital, often refuse to spend it.

This creates a curious paradox: power has never been more carefully cultivated or jealously protected, yet its application has rarely been more constrained. Political energy is consumed not by governing, but by the processes of acquiring, defending and retaining office. It must be exhausting! Meanwhile, the country drifts.

What this reveals is a deeper problem: an atrophy of purpose. Power to function meaningfully in a democratic system must be anchored to a sense of direction. It must have somewhere to go. When political parties no longer know why they want to govern, beyond the goal of simply being in power, then they are left with little to say and even less to do. Governance becomes an exercise in administration, not transformation, which means the politicians largely become superfluous to the administration of the nation.

The public, too, senses the emptiness. Voter disengagement, trust deficits and cynicism are not abstract trends. They are rational responses to a political system that appears more interested in itself than in those it governs. Citizens no longer expect boldness, they hope merely for competence. This dynamic poses a long-term threat to the legitimacy of democratic governance.

Leadership Without Direction

Leadership in Australian politics has undergone a slow but significant transformation. Once grounded in ideology, conviction or a clear sense of national direction, it has become increasingly shaped by the rhythms of the news cycle and the imperatives of political survival. Today's leaders are often judged not by the scale of their vision or the durability of their reform legacy, but by their capacity to manage media appearances. It is leadership stripped of substance.

This shift is not merely a matter of style winning out over substance. It reflects deeper structural changes in the political system. The decline of internal party democracy, the rise of professional political operatives, and the increasing dominance of focus group-driven policymaking have all contributed to a leadership culture largely concerned with impressions. The performative eclipses purpose.

It wasn't always this way. Past leaders tended to arrive in office with an animating agenda. Gough Whitlam's whirlwind of progressive reform, Malcolm Fraser's institutional conservatism, Bob Hawke's economic modernisation, Paul Keating's push for republicanism and reconciliation, John Howard's fusion of liberalism and social conservatism. These were leaders shaped by belief systems, driving coherent policy agendas over time. Disagree or agree with their politics, their leadership was recognisably about something. Even in the case of Fraser his do-nothing administration was an ideological response to the era of Whitlam, which conservatives believed made too many changes too quickly.

In contrast, more recent prime ministers have often struggled to articulate what they stand for beyond generic platitudes. Their public rhetoric is saturated with slogans. The absence of a clear ideological compass leaves them exposed to drift. Their authority is drawn not from a mandate for reform, but from a manufactured perception of control. It is leadership by default.

When leadership lacks direction, it tends to prioritise the management of risk over the pursuit of outcomes. Leaders become stewards of stability to the next election rather than agents of change, even left wing ideologues like Albanese. The goal becomes to "get through" the term without incident. Ministers are discouraged from taking bold initiatives; departmental advice is filtered through political staffers; and policy proposals are tested not for efficacy but for potential controversy. A government's success is measured in terms of surviving the next election, not shaping the next generation.

Even the language of leadership has changed. Where once there was talk of nation-building, structural reform, or grand bargains, today we hear of "optics," "narratives," and "announceables." Leaders speak the language of marketing. For some, like Scott Morrison, it was their pre-parliamentary profession. Their authority is sustained through appearances, not accomplishments. This hollowness is not hidden from the public.

There is also a direct connection between the decline in purposeful leadership and the rise of populism. When mainstream leaders vacate the space of substantive policy debates they create a vacuum that gets filled by opportunists. Without a clear ideological framework, political discourse becomes a free-for-all of competing grievances and simplistic solutions. This fuels disaffection, reinforces cynicism and makes democratic governance even more fragile.

It is telling that some of the more ambitious policy moves in recent years have come not from elected leaders, but from independent institutions or non-governmental actors: central banks pursuing monetary policy innovations, universities shaping research agendas, or even state premiers taking the lead during a national crisis like the COVID-19 pandemic. When federal leadership retreats into caution and obfuscation, others must fill the vacuum.

Governance by Default

As political leadership becomes increasingly directionless, the style of governance it produces shifts accordingly. With little ideological drive or long-term strategic ambition to anchor decision-making, governments default to a mode of administration that is cautious, reactive and sometimes reliant on external actors to do the heavy lifting. Governance becomes a process of ticking boxes not building legacies. It is in every sense governance by default.

The signs are everywhere. Major policy reforms are rare and when they occur they are usually modest in scope and tightly focus-grouped. Long-term planning is outsourced to departmental reviews, independent commissions or consultants. Ministers become portfolio managers rather than policy entrepreneurs, focused on damage control and media strategy rather than legislative impact. Departments, once the intellectual engine rooms of reforms, are hollowed out or sidelined altogether. In the absence of a strong policy agenda, inertia becomes the dominant force in the machinery of government.

This style of governance suits the political class because it reduces the risk of failure. Bold reforms might alienate stakeholders, provoke backlash or backfire at the point of implementation. By contrast, incrementalism provides a veneer of activity without the threat of disruption. This pattern is reinforced by the political incentives that shape the governing process. Success is measured in the avoidance of problems rather than the pursuit of solutions. As a result, governance is increasingly shaped by events rather than guided by plans.

Governance by default is also visible in the growing dependence on legacy systems, outdated frameworks and administrative workarounds. Governments inherit institutional structures that are no longer fit for purpose, yet they rarely engage in the hard work of structural reform. From tax policy to federation arrangements, from housing regulation to climate strategy, inertia dominates. Even when there is political agreement about the need for change, the will to act often evaporates under the pressure of the day-to-day.

This tendency to govern passively contributes to the erosion of public trust. Moreover, governance by default weakens the resilience of the state. When government avoids difficult choices, defers structural reform and contracts out core responsibilities it becomes less capable of responding to future challenges. Institutions are not static; if they are not nurtured they degrade. A state that governs by default is one that slowly but surely hollows out.

The COVID-19 pandemic provided a stark illustration of this dynamic. Faced with a once-in-a-generation crisis, governments were forced to act decisively. In some respects, Australia performed well (particularly at the state level). But the crisis also revealed the fragility of the federal government's internal capacity. Poor coordination, fragmented responsibilities and a lack of clear federal leadership exposed the costs of a system that had been drifting for too long. This is a failure of governance philosophy: Without a vision to guide it the state cannot function as a strategic actor.

Crucially, this model of governance is self-perpetuating. Because governments that govern by default rarely leave a legacy of reform, there is little incentive for successors to do otherwise. New administrations inherit systems that reward caution and punish ambition. They are socialised into a political culture where maintaining equilibrium is valued over shaping outcomes.

Politics without Purpose

Politics, at its best, is a contest of ideas. A means by which societies navigate competing values, balance interests and articulate collective aspirations. It is supposed to be the arena in which decisions of consequence are debated and resolved, grounded in democratic accountability and a sense of civic duty. But in the hollow state politics is increasingly stripped of this moral and intellectual weight. It becomes not a means to an end but an end in itself. The result is purposeless politics: a relentless performance of power without direction.

At the centre of purposeless politics is the professional political class, a group of individuals whose careers are forged within the structures of party politics but who often lack deep ties to policy communities, civil society or ideological traditions. They are rarely qualified for the roles they occupy. These are not political leaders in the traditional sense, they are political operatives supposedly skilled in tactics but disconnected from the public good. They understand how to climb the internal ladder, manipulate the media cycle and navigate factional alliances, but they frequently lack a sense of what politics is ultimately for. Most are callow.

This results in a political culture that prioritises style over substance. The optics of a policy are more important than its efficacy. Public messaging is crafted not to inform or persuade, but to neutralise criticisms and control the narrative. Parliamentary questions are answered evasively, if at all. Press conferences are managed down to the word. When that fails the media picks over the superficial.

In this setting, political debate becomes decoupled from reality. Complex issues are reduced to culture war flashpoints. The media plays a complicit role in amplifying this, focusing on conflict and controversy at the expense of context and clarity. But the responsibility to rise above this circus rests with the political class.

When political discourse no longer aims to grapple with real-world problems, policy stagnation becomes inevitable. The incentives shift away from evidence-based decision-making and toward performative politics. Ministers are rewarded for being on-message, not for reforming broken systems. Shadow ministers echo this style in opposition, perpetuating a cycle of superficiality.

Even within government, this purposelessness creates friction. At its core, purposeless politics reflects a deeper philosophical crisis. It reveals a political class that has lost sight of why it sought power in the first place, if it ever knew. Without a compelling narrative about the future, politics loses its normative force. It cannot inspire, mobilise or unify. It cannot justify sacrifice, demand effort or call forth the better instincts of the electorate. It becomes banal.

What remains is power for power's sake: a hollow prize pursued through hollow means by an unimpressive political class. The machinery of politics continues to grind on, but it no longer produces the civic goods it once promised. This is the ultimate consequence of the hollow state: not just weak institutions or bad policy, but a fundamental erosion of political meaning creating drift.

The Price of Drift

The cumulative effect of power without purpose is not merely a degraded political culture, it is a diminished nation. The price of drift, while not always immediately visible, manifests across the institutions of government, in the policy failures that compound over time, and in the eroded trust that citizens place in the system. When politics ceases to be purposeful, the state itself loses coherence. The consequences are structural, not just symbolic.

In practical terms, drift leads to chronic underperformance in public policy. Reform is repeatedly delayed, even where consensus exists because no one is willing to expend the political capital required to push it through. Long-term challenges are left to fester. When action finally comes it is often reactive, fragmented and insufficient. The state becomes a responder not a planner.

This is particularly damaging in areas requiring long-term investment and political coordination. Infrastructure planning, environmental policy and social services cannot be effectively governed through short-tern politicking. Yet drift ensures precisely that: governments focus on budget cycles not generational horizons. As a result, Australia faces a growing backlog of reform across key sectors, much of it acknowledged but left untouched.

The deterioration of institutional capacity is another cost of drift. Public services once repositories of expertise and engines of innovation, become demoralised and risk-averse. Policy skills atrophy. Institutional knowledge is lost. Senior bureaucrats deprived of meaningful influence either leave or retreat into managerial compliance. The erosion of the public service is not only a function of active political interference, it is also a consequence of neglect. When ministers cease to demand rigorous forward-looking advice, the incentive to provide it disappears.

This same institutional decline is evident in the political parties themselves. As discussed in Chapter 8, parties that once served as vehicles of political vision are now organisational shells, focused more on fundraising and factional dominance than movement-building. The result is a talent pipeline that prioritises loyalty over capability, message discipline over policy fluency. Drift is reinforced by mediocrity.

But perhaps the greatest price of drift is paid by the people. Citizens disengage from a political process they rightly perceive as empty. Voter turnout may remain high by international standards, because of our compulsory voting system, but political literacy and democratic satisfaction are in decline. Surveys routinely show that Australians, particularly younger generations, are losing faith in the efficacy of democratic institutions. They see politics as a game, politicians as players and themselves as spectators, largely powerless to shape outcomes.

This alienation is not abstract, it has tangible consequences. Disengaged citizens are less likely to participate in civil society more generally, and less willing to contribute to public discourse. They are also more susceptible to misinformation and populism. In this environment, the guardrails of democracy weaken.

There is also an opportunity cost to drift. The absence of purposeful politics means lost chances to lead, inspire and shape the national story. Australia is a wealthy, stable and educated country with enormous potential to be a policy innovator on the global stage. Instead, we increasingly follow rather than lead. Even politically expedient achievements are undermined by this drift. When governments do act the absence of narrative coherence weakens legitimacy. Policy lacks the scaffolding of principle, and therefore struggles to endure.

Drift, in this sense, is not a pause in political momentum, it is a gravitational pull away from meaningful governance. It breeds fatalism within institutions and cynicism within the public. And unlike scandal or crisis, which can sometimes shock a system into action, drift is insidious. It is sustained through routine, justified by base pragmatism and rewarded by short-term success.

This chapter has argued that the hollow state is defined by precisely this phenomenon: power wielded for its own sake with little reference to long-term purpose. The institutions of democracy continue to function, but with declining meaning and diminishing effect. So what might come next?

Chapter 14

BEYOND THE HOLLOW STATE

Over the course of this book I have sought to map the contours of a political system that has lost its way. Not in moments of crisis or spectacular failure, but through the steady erosion of purpose, principle and institutional integrity. The hollowing out of the Australian state has been a process. Each preceding chapter has examined a different facet of this transformation, from the rise of a managerial political class to the collapse of conviction and the weakening of the party system.

We have seen how the public service has been depoliticised in theory but politicised in practice, how the fourth estate has retreated under the pressures of a broken business model, and how democracy itself has been undermined. A pattern has emerged: power continues to be exercised, but without the grounding of real purpose.

This chapter does not offer a sweeping solution to these problems. There is no single reform that can reverse decades of drift. Nor does it seek to present a utopian vision of democratic renewal. Instead, it asks what might come next, beyond the hollow state. What possibilities exist, however fragile or remote, for a reconstitution of public purpose in politics? What spaces remain for institutional rebuilding, cultural renewal or new political leadership grounded in principle? And crucially, what lessons can be drawn from the failures of the recent past?

The Limits of Technocracy

The drift into managerialism, traced throughout this book, has left

Australian politics increasingly hollow. Governed more by process than principle, and by the logic of administration rather than the demands of leadership. Nowhere is this more evident than in the rise of technocracy as the default mode of governance, not that politicians are even experts in the fields they oversee. Nonetheless, complex policy challenges are recast as technical problems with data-driven solutions. Political actors position themselves not as representatives of moral or ideological traditions, but as competent managers of risk. In this framing the appearance of control trumps the exercising of convictions.

There is, of course, a place for expertise and evidence in policymaking. Effective governance depends on access to sound advice, accurate information and robust systems of evaluation. But when technocratic thinking becomes dominant and the tools of government are confused with its purpose, the political system loses the capacity to engage in moral arguments or long-term vision. Politics becomes a case of tinkering with levers, not deciding where to go next.

This technocratic impulse has been particularly prominent in recent decades, as governments have responded to globalisation, economic volatility and rapid technological changes. In many cases politicians have outsourced key functions of governance to "experts" not only within the bureaucracy but increasingly to consultants, think tanks and private actors. Political leadership becomes less about setting a course and more about managing complexity. This suits a political class reluctant to articulate values let alone fight for them.

The COVID-19 pandemic revealed both the strengths and limits of technocracy. On the one hand governments rightly deferred to medical and scientific experts in navigating public health responses. On the other hand those same governments often failed to embed technical decisions within a coherent social or political framework. The language of "following the health advice" became a substitute for leadership, not a complement to it. Crucial decisions about rights, responsibilities and resource allocations were framed as administrative rather than democratic questions.

This reliance on expertise also leaves governments exposed when things go wrong. If a policy is sold purely on the grounds of technical efficiency, there is little political cover when it proves inadequate or unjust, much less wrong. By outsourcing both responsibility and rationale political leaders insulate themselves in the short term but erode trust over time.

Moreover, technocratic politics struggles with contestation. Because it assumes that problems have objectively correct solutions, it finds disagreement uncomfortable, even illegitimate. But democracy thrives on conflict. Not destructive partisanship, but the contest of ideas, values and interests. Reducing this to a competition between spreadsheets and dashboards hollows out the democratic project itself.

In the Australian context, this has contributed to a narrowing of political discourse. Big-picture debates are sidelined in favour of incremental adjustments. Reform is endlessly delayed, not because there is no knowledge of what needs to be done, but because the system is unwilling to bear the political cost of doing it. The machinery of government hums along, producing white papers and reviews, but rarely charting a course forward by implementing the guts of what gets proposed.

To move beyond the hollow state will require more than technocratic competence. It requires a reassertion of politics as a realm of purpose, where decisions are contested on ethical as well as practical grounds, and where leadership involves making difficult choices in full view of the public. Technocracy, left unchecked, becomes a form of quiet authoritarianism. Its seduction lies in its promise of neutrality, but in reality it is deeply political and all the more dangerous for pretending not to be.

Restoring Democratic Legitimacy

Legitimacy is the cornerstone of any democratic system. Without it institutions cannot command the authority they require to govern effectively, nor can elected representatives claim to act with the consent of the governed. In Australia, as in many established democracies, legitimacy has been quietly slipping away. The symptoms are now familiar. The problems are not surface level, they are structural and go to the heart of democratic decline.

One of the core arguments running through this book has been that Australian democracy is not broken in the way populists or extremists often claim. It is functioning but has become increasingly detached from any substantive vision. Electoral contests still take place, parliament still sits and laws are still passed. Yet the underlying sense that these processes are meaningful is what is in retreat. People no longer believe that elections significantly alter the trajectory of public policy. As a consequence they lose meaning for all but the players themselves who are fighting over the trinkets of power.

This crisis of legitimacy is intimately linked to the managerialism described in earlier chapters. When politics is reduced to administration there is little for citizens to connect to beyond performance metrics and service delivery. The idea of politics as a shared democratic project rooted in values and competing visions gives way to a model of passive consumption. Voters are treated as clients rather than citizens.

The hollowing out of the party system has further undermined its legitimacy. With mass party membership now a relic of the past, political parties no longer function as vehicles for public participation. The media has also played a role, with the fourth estate retreating from its watchdog function, becoming an echo chamber for the political class or a platform for sensationalism.

Restoring legitimacy is not simply a matter of better messaging or improved transparency. It requires a fundamental rethinking of the relationship between citizens and the state. This begins with participation, not just through elections but in decision-making processes that affect people's lives. Participatory budgeting, citizens' assemblies and deliberative forums are not panaceas, but they signal a willingness to involve people in shaping outcomes, not just reacting to them. Where they have been tried they tend to build trust, increase satisfaction with governance and generate more nuanced policy outcomes. This could be a major part of rebuilding democratic legitimacy.

Legitimacy is also rebuilt through representation. A political class that reflects the diversity of the country (across gender, race, class and geography) is more likely to be seen as legitimate. But representation is not just about identity politicking. Representatives must be embedded in their communities not simply parachuted in by party powerbrokers having ticked certain boxes.

Institutional reform matters too. Restoring trust requires revisiting the checks and balances that underpin democratic government: strengthening integrity bodies, ensuring genuine parliamentary scrutiny and removing the undue influence of money in politics are just some of the things that might need to happen. These are not abstract concerns, they shape how people perceive the fairness and responsiveness of the political system.

Education is another long-term lever to restore democratic legitimacy. Lteracy is alarmingly low in Australia, and this feeds into disengagement. When citizens do not understand how government works they are less able to demand accountability or imagine alternatives. Reinvigorating and modernising civics education, from schools to adult programs, should be a national priority.

Finally, leadership matters. Legitimacy is fragile and it can be rebuilt or destroyed by how leaders behave. Integrity, honesty and humility in public office are not quaint ideals, they are essential for maintaining public confidence. When leaders admit error, engage openly, and resist the temptation of spin they reinforce democratic norms. When they do the opposite, the damage is cumulative.

In short, legitimacy cannot be manufactured by communications strategies or symbolic gestures. It must be earned. As Australia confronts the consequences of a hollowed-out political system, if indeed it ever does confront it, the restoration of democratic legitimacy will be both a test and a precondition of renewal.

Are Parties Past Repair?

Political parties are meant to be the connective tissue of representative democracy. In theory they are supposed to be vehicles of democratic participation and ideological clarity. In practice, however, they have become hollow institutions detached from their memberships and increasingly indistinguishable in terms of policy and purpose. The Australian experience is emblematic of a broader crisis facing centre-left and centre-right parties across advanced democracies. The question is no longer whether political parties are failing, it is whether they are capable of real reform.

As explored in Chapter 8, mass party organisations have dwindled into hollow professionalised organisations. Membership numbers are at historic lows. Party branches are no longer spaces of grassroots activism or political education, but battlegrounds for factional control used to secure preselections. The average citizen has no meaningful entry point into party politics anymore. The parties themselves have become increasingly reliant on professional operatives — pollsters, campaign consultants and strategists — who view politics as a game to be won rather than a contest of ideas to be celebrated.

This professionalisation has consequences. It hollows out internal democracy, concentrates power in a handful of backroom actors and elevates short-term tactics over long-term purpose. Party conferences and policy debates are stage-managed affairs. Backbenchers toe the line or risk career stagnation. Leadership contests are often determined by factional numbers not public support or intellectual authority. The result is a political class that appears more loyal to its internal alliances than to any coherent policy program. Loyalty to the tribe matters more than leadership of the nation.

Ideologically, the parties have converged in Australia. The policy space between major parties has narrowed, particularly on economic issues. Both major parties have embraced market-based solutions, small-target strategies and risk-averse politics. Both are now spending uncontrollably, in increasing violation of some of these earlier agreed principles. There is little appetite for structural reform and almost no willingness to challenge entrenched interests.

Internally reform efforts have largely failed. Token gestures toward greater member participation, such as giving rank-and-file members a say in leadership elections, are often undermined by factional control or quietly reversed when inconvenient. Genuine democratic reforms within parties would require confronting entrenched interests, challenging long-standing networks of patronage and rethinking the very nature of political organisation in the 21st century. Few party leaders have shown the courage or imagination to pursue such change.

Externally a reliance on corporate donations and lobbyist influence has deepened public scepticism towards political parties. Campaign finance reform remains piecemeal. Transparency regimes are still weak. The major parties' dependence on external money not only compromises their independence but also erodes their claim to legitimacy.

Some defenders of the status quo argue that parties remain essential to governance and must therefore be preserved. Perhaps. But preservation is not the same as renewal. If parties are to survive as relevant institutions they must find a way to reconnect with the public, not through spin or rebranding but via genuine democratic engagement. They must once again become places where ideas are contested and where membership matters.

At present the signs are not promising. The party system continues to stumble along more concerned with internal control than external relevance. For now, parties are still the main vehicles for forming governments. But their legitimacy is in decline, their social base is crumbling and their purpose is somewhat opaque. In many ways they are already past repair: Whether they can (or should) be saved remains one of the defining questions of Australia's political future.

Can Institutions Be Rebuilt?

If the hollowing out of Australia's political institutions is well documented then the natural question is whether these institutions can be renewed or meaningfully repurposed. The answer is not straightforward. Institutions by their very nature are slow-moving. They do not change with the pace of electoral cycles, and they resist reform unless pressured by sustained public demand or systemic failure. Yet institutions also endure. They carry the potential for renewal even if that potential is latent and underutilised. The question is not whether institutional renewal is possible, it is whether it is likely in the current political environment.

The Australian public sector was once a focal point of national pride. It was staffed by experts, respected for its independence and structured to provide robust evidence-based advice to governments of all persuasions. But decades of politicisation, outsourcing, and managerialism have weakened its capacity and morale. Rebuilding the public service means more than restoring technical expertise, it includes reasserting the value of impartial advice, empowering senior officials to speak truth to power and re-establishing a culture of public service that is independent rather than subservient.

Parliament's deliberative quality has suffered. Question Time is theatre, not scrutiny. Committee work is often undermined by partisan behaviour or derailed by headline grabbing antics. The dominance of the executive, particularly the Prime Minister's Office, has left Parliament diminished in both practice and perception. Restoring parliamentary strength would require genuine respect for process: allowing more free votes, enhancing committee independence and empowering crossbench contributions. It also means resisting the trend toward centralised power and the politics of spin, which have contributed so heavily to the erosion of institutional credibility.

Importantly, rebuilding institutions is not simply a technical or procedural exercise. It is also cultural. Institutions reflect the values of those who inhabit and lead them. A Parliament filled with hyper-partisan actors will not magically become deliberative. A bureaucracy led by those looking for post-political sinecures will not champion fearless advice. Reform requires more than structural redesign, it demands a redefinition of norms and expectations. Culture is shaped by incentives, leadership and public pressure. Without these institutional reform risks becoming a tick-box exercise: change without substance.

Finally, the challenge of rebuilding institutions must be understood in the context of political will. Reform is not new, many of the ideas floated here have been recommended by expert panels, parliamentary inquiries and academics for years now. What has been lacking is the courage to act. The political incentives to preserve the status quo remain strong, particularly for those already in positions of power.

And yet moments of institutional renewal do occur. The post-Whitlam reforms of the 1970s, for example, redefined public accountability and transparency. The electoral and party finance reforms of the 1980s and 90s marked another high point. There is precedent for change, but it requires political bravery, media support and civic mobilisation.

So, can institutions be rebuilt? The short answer is yes, but only if there is a sustained effort to do so. The alternative is not stasis but continued decline, where hollow institutions become not just dysfunctional but actively corrosive to democracy.

The Leadership Vacuum

If institutions are the architecture of democracy, leadership is its lifeblood. No amount of reform or structural tinkering will succeed without individuals willing to exercise courage, vision and responsibility. Yet one of the defining characteristics of the hollow state is the absence of precisely this kind of leadership. Across successive governments, at both federal and state levels, Australia has witnessed a drift toward managerialism and political cowardice. Leaders have become risk-averse administrators, more comfortable navigating daily headlines than setting long-term agendas.

This vacuum is not accidental. It is the product of the systemic shifts described throughout this book: the rise of the political class, the collapse of internal party democracy, the decline of robust public debate and the increasing dominance of media spin. Together, these forces have created an environment in which authentic leadership is discouraged. Politicians who speak plainly or act decisively risk alienation.

As discussed in Chapter 7, modern political leaders often leave office with little in the way of an enduring legacy. Policy achievements, when they exist, are modest or technocratic. There is a palpable reluctance to pursue reform that might alienate powerful interests or polarise voters. Instead, governments focus on short-term deliverables, symbolic gestures, or 'announceables' designed to generate positive coverage. Leadership is measured not by impact, but by longevity. The fact this marker of success now also is held up as a goal of itself on the progressive side of politics tells us everything about the loss of convictions and purpose in parliament.

Moreover, the absence of genuine leadership has a corrosive effect on public trust. Voters sense the hollowness. They see the empty slogans, the tactical manoeuvring and the lack of follow-through. Cynicism grows when politicians over-promise and under-deliver, when rhetoric outpaces reality and when no one is really ever held accountable. The credibility gap between political speeches and political action widens. In such an environment even the best institutional reforms will struggle to gain traction.

That is not to say that all hope is lost. There have been exceptions, leaders who have broken through the noise to articulate a clear vision. Or who have stood firm in the face of opposition. But they remain exceptions. More often, politics continues to reward the cautious over the courageous. In some cases, the few who do take risks find themselves politically isolated or electorally punished, further disincentivising others from following in their shoes.

The challenge is to recalibrate our expectations of leadership. This is not about lionising individuals or seeking messianic figures. It is about creating the conditions under which leadership can flourish: internal party cultures that value merit over loyalty; media environments that reward substance over spin; public conversations that allow for complexity rather than just simplicity.

Ultimately, the hollow state is as much a leadership crisis as it is an institutional one. Without individuals prepared to use power with purpose, even the most well-constructed systems will falter. The renewal of Australian democracy depends not just on rebuilding structures, but on reimagining what leadership can and should be. Until we do that, the vacuum at the heart of the system will continue to undermine the body politic.

Democracy's Tipping Point?

Democracy is not guaranteed. Its endurance depends on the vitality of its institutions, the integrity of its leaders and the participation of citizens. When these elements weaken simultaneously, as they have here in Australia, democracy begins to tip from resilience into fragility. This final chapter has explored whether the system can be renewed. But even the possibility of renewal presupposes that we are not already too far down the path of democratic erosion. It is in this context that we must consider whether Australia's democracy is approaching, or has perhaps already crossed, a tipping point.

Throughout this book I have charted the incremental decay of democratic norms and structures: the rise of a managerial political class, the collapse of internal party democracy, the weakening of the public service, the transformation of the media and the strategic cynicism that defines modern political leadership. Taken individually, these developments may appear manageable. Taken together they reveal a systemic rot.

At the heart of this decay is a loss of democratic legitimacy. Citizens increasingly feel that their voices do not matter, that politicians are unresponsive and that the system is rigged in favour of vested interests. There is a growing risk that Australians disengage not just from individual political parties or issues, but from the democratic process itself. When politics is seen as theatre, leaders as actors and policies as mere props, then citizens lose the sense that democracy is a meaningful exercise they should involve themselves in. This is the hollow state in its most dangerous form.

The tipping point, then, is not marked by a single event. It is reached through the cumulative effect of a thousand small failures each one weakening the civic fabric. When lies go unchallenged, when corruption is excused, when accountability is performative rather than substantive, the public simply grows numb. Trust is eroded slowly and rebuilt only with great difficulty.

And yet the tipping point is not inevitable. It can be resisted. Democratic decline can be arrested and reversed, if there is a collective will to do so. That requires more than institutional reform or policy adjustment. It demands a cultural shift. Such a shift cannot come solely from the top. Political leaders may initiate change, but citizens must demand it. Civil society, unions, universities, the media, and community groups alongside private organisations all have a role to play. So too does every voter. A passive electorate is a politician's dream but democracy's nightmare.

Whether Australia is past the point of no return remains an open question. But one thing is clear: the longer we wait to act, the harder it will be to recover what has been lost. The hollow state cannot sustain a vibrant democracy indefinitely.

BIBLIOGRAPHY

1. Bongiorno, F. (2022). Dreamers and Schemers: A Political History of Australia. La Trobe University Press.

2. Brackertz, N. (2013). Political actor or policy instrument? Governance challenges in Australian local government. Commonwealth Journal of Local Governance, (12), 3–19.

3. Brennan, G., & Castles, F. G. (2002). Australia Reshaped: 200 Years of Institutional Transformation. Cambridge University Press.

4. Brett, J. (2019). From Secret Ballot to Democracy Sausage: How Australia Got Compulsory Voting. Text Publishing.

5. Chalmers, J. (2013). Glory Daze: How a World-beating Nation Got So Down on Itself. Melbourne University Publishing.

6. Dowding, K., & Martin, A. (2016). Policy Agendas in Australia. Palgrave Macmillan.

7. Errington, W., & van Onselen, P. (2015). The Turnbull Gamble. Melbourne University Publishing.

8. Fenna, A. (2019). The centralization of Australian federalism 1901–2010: Measurement and interpretation. Publius: The Journal of Federalism, 49(1), 30–56.

9. Freeman, D. (2024). The End of Settlement: Why the 2023 Referendum Failed. [Publisher unspecified].

10. Gauja, A. (2015). Policy development in political parties. In B. Head & K. Crowley (Eds.), Policy Analysis in Australia (pp. 201–216). Policy Press.

11. Grattan Institute. (2021). Policy paralysis is constraining Australian prosperity. Grattan Institute.

12. Hamilton, C. (2018). Silent Invasion: China's Influence in Australia. Hardie Grant.

13. Hamilton, C., & Maddison, S. (Eds.). (2007). Silencing Dissent: How the Australian Government is Controlling Public Opinion and Stifling Debate. Allen & Unwin.

14. Kefford, G., Murphy-Gregory, H., Ward, I., Jackson, S., Cox, L., & Carson, A. (2018). Australian Politics in the Twenty-First Century: Old Institutions, New Challenges. Cambridge University Press.

15. Kay, A. (2017). Policy failures, policy learning and institutional change: The case of Australian health insurance policy change. Policy and Politics, 45(1), 87–101.

16. Kelly, P. (2014). Triumph and Demise: The Broken Promise of a Labor Generation. Melbourne University Publishing.

17. Kelly, S. (2021). The Game: A Portrait of Scott Morrison. Black Inc.

18. Manne, R. (Ed.). (2011). The Words That Made Australia: How a Nation Came to Know Itself. Black Inc.

19. Marsh, I., & Yencken, D. (2004). Into the hollow state: Capacity and legitimacy in contemporary governance. Australian Journal of Public Administration, 63(2), 66–79.

20. McKenzie, M. (2018). The erosion of minimum wage policy in Australia and labour's shrinking share of total income. Journal of Australian Political Economy, (81), 52–77.

21. Megalogenis, G. (2012). The Australian Moment: How We Were Made for These Times. Penguin.

22. Perche, D., Barry, N., Fenna, A., Ghazarian, Z., & Haigh, Y. (2024). Australian Politics and Policy: Senior Edition. Sydney University Press.

23. Rhodes, R. A. W. (2011). Everyday Life in British Government. Oxford University Press.

24. Sawer, M., Abjorensen, N., & Larkin, P. (2009). Australia: The State of Democracy. Federation Press.

25. Schultz, J. (2022). The Idea of Australia: A Search for the Soul of the Nation. Allen & Unwin.

26. Smith, R., Vromen, A., & Cook, I. (2012). Contemporary Politics in Australia: Theories, Issues and Debates. Cambridge University Press.

27. Stoker, G., & Evans, M. (2016). Political science, governance and the hollowing out of democracy. Australian Journal of Political Science, 51(2), 182–194.

28. van Onselen, P., & Errington, W. (2007). John Winston Howard: The Biography. Melbourne University Publishing.

29. Wallace, C. (2020). Political Lives: Australian Prime Ministers and Their Biographers. UNSW Press.

30. Walter, J. (2010). Policy churn and the politics of expertise in Australia. Australian Journal of Public Administration, 69(2), 165–177.

31. Ward, I. (2017). Political communication in Australia: Breaking down the barriers. In Simms, M. (Ed.), Transforming Politics: The Impact of the Digital Revolution (pp. 55–73). ANU Press.

32. Wanna, J. (2020). Public service reform in Australia: Continuity and change. Australian Journal of Public Administration, 79(3), 309–319.

33. Johnson, C. (2016). Turnbull's centrism and the limits of leadership. Australian Quarterly, 87(1), 4–9.

34. Parkin, A., & Anderson, G. (2007). Federalism: Placing Australian democracy in context. In Warhurst, J., & Simms, M. (Eds.), Democracy in Australia (pp. 93–111). Federation Press.

35. Tiernan, A., & Weller, P. (2010). Learning to be a minister: Heroic expectations, practical realities. Melbourne University Publishing.

36. Hollier, N. (Ed.). (2019). Australian Politics in the Twenty-First Century: Old Institutions, New Challenges. The Meanjin Papers.

37. Curthoys, A., & Ward, R. (2010). Who Are We?: Australia's National Identity. Black Inc.

38. Brett, J. (2021). The mysterious case of the disappearing voter. The Monthly, April.

39. Kenny, M. (2014). The rise of career politicians in Australia. Australian Journal of Political Science, 49(3), 395–407.

40. Gauja, A. (2013). The Politics of Party Policy: From Members to Legislators. Palgrave Macmillan.

41. Uhr, J. (2005). Terms of Trust: Arguments over Ethics in Australian Government. UNSW Press.

42. Costar, B., & Economou, N. (2004). The 2004 federal election: Coalition consolidation. Australian Journal of Political Science, 40(2), 315–326.

43. Head, B. W. (2010). Reconsidering evidence-based policy: Key issues and challenges. Policy and Society, 29(2), 77–94.

44. Goot, M. (2018). Public opinion and Australian political culture. In Johnson, C. & Wanna, J. (Eds.), The Rudd Government (pp. 23–38). ANU Press.

45. Stewart, J. (2012). The political science of austerity. Australian Journal of Political Science, 47(2), 181–193.

46. Rundle, G. (2016). Hollowing out: The political class and the decline of public purpose. Quarterly Essay, (61).

ACKNOWLEDGMENTS

This book would not exist without the support, insight and encouragement of those closest to me.

To Ainslie, thank you for your unwavering support, patience and perspective, not just throughout the writing of this book, but over the many years leading up to it. You've always understood the strange pull of political writing, and you've never asked me to step back from it. Your steadiness and sharpness are everywhere in these pages, even if your name appears only here.

To Sasha and Chloe, you are the daily reminders that there's so much more to life than one's work. Watching you grow into fierce, thoughtful young women has been the greatest privilege of all.

A heartfelt thanks to Michael Wilkinson at the publisher's desk. This project might have started as yet another pile of notes and frustrations, but it became a book because you believed in it and kept coming back to me to pull it all together. Paul Marcolin brought elegance and order not just to the layout, but to the entire visual identity of the book. That he managed to capture the tone of a "hollow state" on the cover without it feeling hollow itself is no small feat. Thanks too to Jane Wilkinson, whose close reading and thoughtful suggestions sharpened the manuscript at key moments. Every book needs someone willing to challenge a sentence rather than just admire it, Jane was that person. I would also like to thank Cassie Chiong for doing the final proofread of the manuscript ahead of page setting and catching a few of my clangers!

There's always a teacher. For me, it was Mr Sergio Sergi, my high school English teacher who was the first to suggest that writing and politics might be more than just distractions from business and economics. When I drifted into university on the back of time in his classroom, he reminded me where my interests actually lay, and gave me the encouragement I needed to pursue them. This book and the others I have written owe more to him than he probably realises.

Finally, a quiet note on process. In assembling this book, I made limited use of artificial intelligence tools for the very first time, to assist with referencing and editing. I guess you can teach an old dog new tricks! In a sense AI became my research assistant for this project, which has made me think harder about what its potential impact on the jobs of the future might be. Used responsibly it may yet help improve the quality of public discourse, including in politics and policymaking, which is at the heart of this book's subject matter. But it also presents new challenges that will only come into sharper focus as this century roles on.

Despite all the help, guidance and encouragement I've had in writing this manuscript, all remaining errors are of course my own.